**Scott, Foresman
Basics in Reading**

# Ride a Rainbow

**Program Authors**

Ira E. Aaron
Dauris Jackson
Carole Riggs
Richard G. Smith
Robert Tierney

**Book Authors**

Ira E. Aaron
Rena Koke

**Instructional
Consultant**

John Manning

Scott, Foresman and Company
Editorial Offices: Glenview, Illinois

Regional Sales Offices: Palo Alto,
California • Tucker, Georgia • Glenview
Illinois • Oakland, New Jersey • Dallas,
Texas

## Consultants

May Arakaki

Maria Eugenia Matute–Bianchi

Maria Bilbao

Delphina B. Briscoe

Deborah Flores

Jesse Garcia

Evangeline Geiger

Gordon Gray

Barbara Griffin

Barbara Hansen

Jerry A. Rainwater

Betty Robeson

Ann Semel

Joan Takada

Michiko Ikegami Totman

Evelynn Washington

## Acknowledgments

page 35: WIDE WORLD PHOTOS

pages 36–37: DUFFY HAMBLETON

page 38: UPI

page 39: DUFFY HAMBLETON

pages 52–55: Photographs copyright © 1976 by Arthur Sirdofsky.

page 56: Earl L. Kubis, R/C PHOTO AGENCY.

page 60: Jerry Cooke, ANIMALS ANIMALS

page 62 left: Leonard L. T. Rhodes, ANIMALS ANIMALS

page 62 center: Fran Allan, ANIMALS ANIMALS

page 62 right: ANIMALS ANIMALS

pages 78–79: CAMERA 5

page 80 left: CAMERA 5

page 80 right and 81 top: UPI

page 82: Jerome Kresch from PETER ARNOLD

pages 96–100: Chicago Zoological Society

page 162: Jack Stewart, THE SEA LIBRARY

pages 197–198: Photos of Dr. Haycock Courtesy of Dr. Haycock

page 263: Index of American Design, National Gallery of Art, Washington

# Contents

## Section One

4

## Section Two

# Section One

# One Word, Many Meanings

Meg is the sportswriter for her classroom paper. She wrote this story about the baseball game played by the Redbirds and the Bluebirds.

**Bluebirds Win Diamond Championship**
**by Meg Chan**

The strong arm of pitcher Andy King helped the Bluebirds beat the Redbirds 7 to 1. The game had been a 1 to 1 tie until the third inning.

Kim Fowler was the first batter for the Bluebirds in the third inning. She hit the second pitch into the stands for a home run.

The next batter hit a fly that was trapped by the Redbirds' center fielder for the first out. Then Jan Merton hit a ball into left field. She rounded the bases for an inside-the-park home run. And the Bluebirds were ahead 3 to 1.

The Redbirds never scored another run. The Bluebirds scored 4 more runs to win 7 to 1.

8

## Think about skills

Some of the words Meg used in her story have more than one meaning. You can often tell what a word means by using the clues you find as you read.

You know that Meg wrote about a baseball game. So when Meg wrote about a *pitcher,* did she mean
—a container for holding liquids, or
—a person who throws the ball to the batter?
The other words in the story helped you know that Meg was using the second meaning for *pitcher.*

You can also get clues to the meaning of a word from the way it is used in a sentence. Two meanings of the word *fly* are
—move through the air with wings, or
—a ball batted high in the air.

In the next sentence, *fly* means a ball batted high in the air. One of the batters hit a fly into center field.

1. Two meanings of *diamond* are
—a precious stone that is often worn in a ring, or
—the space inside the lines that connect the bases in baseball.

What does *diamond* mean in the next sentence?
Keith lost the diamond when he was swimming.

2. Two meanings of the word *tie* are
—fasten with string, or
—a game in which both teams have the same number of points.

What does *tie* mean in the next sentence?
Laura helped Tony tie the package.

## Practice skills

Read each sentence below. Decide which meaning fits the way in which the underlined word is used in the sentence.

1. My kitten likes to run and <u>play</u> outside.
   a. have fun
   b. a story acted on stage
2. I bought a picture at the art <u>fair</u>.
   a. honest
   b. a show of things people have made
3. Chuck can't go out because he has a <u>cold</u>.
   a. chilly
   b. a common sickness

10

# HOW IS A TABLE LIKE YOU?

by Cynthia Basil

What does a table have that you have?

Legs! A table stands on four legs. You stand on two legs.

Some table legs end with feet. Your legs end with feet.

**What has elbows but no arms?**

The pipes in the kitchen. Elbow is the name for a part of a pipe with a bend.

Some macaroni has a bend too. It is called elbow macaroni.

**What do your head and a clock have in front?**

*1: Apply*

A face! What else does a clock have that you have? Two hands. A clock's hands point to the time on its face. Your hands can point anywhere.

A clock's face has no eyes, no nose, and no mouth. But your face has.

A potato has eyes, but no face. A potato's eyes can't see. Your eyes can.

**What do you have in your mouth that a comb and a saw also have?**

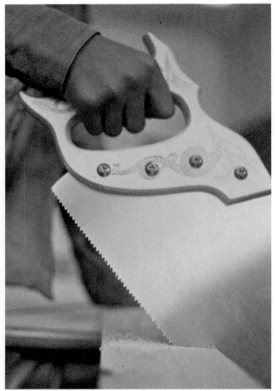

Teeth! A comb's teeth and a saw's teeth are in a row. Your teeth are in a row.

Most combs and saws have only one row of teeth. You have two rows.

A saw's teeth cut wood. Your teeth cut food.

**A road has something that you have too. What is it?**

14

Shoulders. A road's shoulders are at its sides. Your shoulders are at the sides of your neck.

**What does a car have that you have?**

A body!

A car's body and your body are made of many parts, but they have different names. Parts of some things and parts of you have the same names because in some ways they are alike. But nothing is exactly like you!

16

## Think about the selection

1. How is a table like you?
2. How does the picture on page 11 show how a table is like you?
3. Turn to the table of contents on page 3. What story is listed after "How Is a Table Like You?"
4. How is a chair like you?

## Checkpoint 1

1. Each of the words below has more than one meaning. Use each of these words in sentences that show that you know the meanings of these words.

   face    elbow    teeth

2. What is the meaning of *down* in this sentence?
   The cat jumped down from the fence.
   a. soft feathers
   b. to a lower place

# What's the Word?

As you read, you may sometimes come to a word you don't know. The word may be one that you have heard. But you may not have seen the word before. How can you tell what the word is?

**»** If you see a word you don't know in a sentence, try to think of a word that would make sense in the sentence. Then check to see if the consonant sounds in your word match the printed word. **«**

Can you read all the words in the next sentence?

I like to eat beef better than <u>chicken.</u>

You probably know what the underlined word means. But it might be a word you've never seen. What are some words that would make sense in the sentence?

*Pork, turkey,* and *chicken* all make sense in the sentence. But the consonants in *pork* and *turkey* do not match the consonants in the underlined word. The consonants in *chicken* do match. So the underlined word is *chicken.*

18

Which of the three words below each sentence makes the best sense in the blank?

1. Roger likes to write _____.
   a. desks    b. poems    c. hats
2. Barbara goes _____ every day.
   a. shoes    b. sharp    c. swimming

## Practice skills

Which of the three words below each sentence makes the best sense in the blank?

1. My baby brother cries when he is _____.
   a. sometimes    b. hungry    c. have
2. Gerry plays baseball in the _____.
   a. park    b. dark    c. push
3. Frank is taking guitar _____.
   a. lakes    b. lessons    c. lamps
4. Karla is always asking _____.
   a. chairs    b. keys    c. questions

# Ira Sleeps Over

by Bernard Waber

I was invited to sleep at
Reggie's house. Was I happy!
I had never slept at a friend's
house before.

But I had a problem. It
began when my sister said,
"Are you taking your teddy
bear along?"

"Taking my teddy bear!"
I said. "Are you kidding?
That's the silliest thing I ever
heard!"

Then she said, "But you
never slept without your teddy
bear before. How will you
feel sleeping without him
for the very first time?
Hmmmmmmmmm?"

*2: Apply*

"I'll feel fine. I'll feel
great. Just don't worry
about it," I said.

"Who's worried?" she said.

But now she had me
thinking about it. I began to
wonder. Suppose I just hate
sleeping without my teddy
bear? Should I take him?

"Take him," said my
mother.

"Take him," said my father.

"But Reggie will laugh,"
I said. "He'll say I'm a baby."

"He won't laugh," said my
mother.

"He won't laugh," said my
father.

"He'll laugh," said my
sister.

I decided not to take my
teddy bear.

That afternoon I played with Reggie. "Tonight," he said, "we are going to have fun, fun, fun. I'll show you all the junk I've saved. Then we'll have a wrestling match. And after that, a pillow fight."

"Great!" I said. "I can hardly wait. And by the way, what do you think of teddy bears?"

But Reggie just went on talking and planning. "And after that," he said, "do you know what we can do when the house is really dark?"

"What?" I asked.

"We can tell stories. Terrible, scary ghost stories," Reggie said.

I began to think about my teddy bear. "By the way," I said again, "what do you think of teddy bears?"

Suddenly Reggie was in a big hurry to go home.

"See you tonight," he said.

I decided to take my teddy bear.

"Good," said my mother.

"Good," said my father.

But my sister said, "What if Reggie wants to know your teddy bear's name? Did you think about how he will laugh and say Tah Tah is a silly, baby name?"

"He won't ask," I said.

"He'll ask," she said.

I decided not to take my teddy bear.

At last it was time to go to Reggie's house. I went next door where Reggie lived.

Reggie showed me all his junk. After that we had a wrestling match. After that, a pillow fight. And after that Reggie's father said, "Time for bed!"

24

We got into bed. Reggie began to tell a story. "Once there was this ghost," Reggie said. "He lived in a big, old house. Nobody wanted to go near this house. They were afraid. The ghost would go around looking for people to scare. That's what he liked to do—scare people. Oh, was he scary to look at!"

Reggie stopped. "Are you scared?" he asked.

"Yes," I said. "Are you?"

"Just a minute," he said. "I have to get something."

Reggie pulled something out of a drawer. The room was dark, but I could see that the something was fuzzy. It was about the size of a teddy bear.

"Is that your teddy bear?" I asked.

"What?" said Reggie.

"Is that your teddy bear?" I asked again.

"Yes," said Reggie.

"Does your teddy bear have a name?" I asked.

"You won't laugh?" said Reggie.

"No, I won't laugh," I said.

"His name is Foo Foo," said Reggie.

"Did you say Foo Foo?" I asked.

"Yes," said Reggie.

"Just a minute," I said. "I have to get something."

The next minute I was ringing my own
doorbell. "Ira!" everyone said. "What are you
doing here?"

"I decided to take Tah Tah after all," I said.
Then I went upstairs and got Tah Tah.

My sister said, "Reggie will laugh. You'll see.
He's just going to fall down laughing."

"He won't laugh," said my mother.

"He won't laugh," said my father.

"He won't laugh," I said.

2: Apply

I came back to Reggie's room. "I have a teddy bear too," I said. "Do you want to know his name?"

I waited for Reggie to say yes. But he didn't say anything. He was fast asleep.

"Reggie! Wake up!" I said. "You have to finish telling the ghost story!"

But Reggie just held his teddy bear closer and went right on sleeping.

And after that—well, there wasn't anything to do after that. "Good night," I whispered to Tah Tah. And I fell asleep too.

# PEANUTS®

## Think about the selection

1. What was Ira's problem in the story "Ira Sleeps Over"?
2. Do you think Reggie had a problem too? Why do you think as you do?
3. How was Ira's problem solved?
4. What do you think about the way the writer of the story solved Ira's problem? Can you think of other ways the writer could have solved it?
5. In the first cartoon on page 30, how is the girl, Sally, like Ira in "Ira Sleeps Over"?
6. Why does the second cartoon make you think of "Ira Sleeps Over"?
7. How did Linus solve his problem?
8. What do you think of Linus's solution to his problem? Tell why you think as you do.

## Checkpoint 2

Which of the three words below each sentence makes the best sense in the blank?

1. I was ___ to sleep at Reggie's house.
   a. indoors      b. invited      c. indeed
2. That's the ___ thing I ever heard of.
   a. selfish      b. seacoast      c. silliest
3. Don't ___ about me.
   a. worry      b. wormy      c. wobbly
4. I ___ to take my teddy bear.
   a. dandelion      b. delivery      c. decided
5. Reggie pulled something ___ out of a drawer.
   a. fuzzy      b. fruit      c. flag
6. We had a pillow fight, then we ___.
   a. wintered      b. wrestled      c. wrinkled

# Meet the Gerbil

**Carla has a new pet. It is a gerbil. Carla's gerbil has soft fur and large eyes. It is only five inches long. Its back legs are long, and it jumps around like a tiny kangaroo. Carla's gerbil has a long tail with a lot of hair at the tip of it.**

### Think about skills

The main idea of "Meet the Gerbil" is what Carla's gerbil looks like. This is the main idea because it is what the paragraph is about.

One of the sentences says that Carla's gerbil has soft fur and large eyes. This is called a supporting detail because it tells more about the main idea.

But not all the sentences in "Meet the Gerbil" are supporting details. The first sentence says that Carla has a new pet. This is not a supporting detail because it does not tell more about the main idea. It does not tell what Carla's gerbil looks like.

*3: Teach*

Carla keeps her gerbil in a cage. She feeds it different kinds of food. Carla's gerbil eats seeds and gerbil food. And it eats lettuce too. Sometimes, as a treat, Carla feeds the gerbil an apple slice. And she always makes sure that the gerbil has fresh water.

1. Which sentence tells the main idea of the paragraph above?
   a. Carla keeps her gerbil in a cage.
   b. Carla's gerbil eats many kinds of food.
   c. Carla's gerbil likes to eat lettuce.
2. Which two sentences are details that support the main idea?
   a. Carla keeps her gerbil in a cage.
   b. Carla's gerbil eats lettuce.
   c. The gerbil likes apple slices.

## Practice skills

Diane has a paper route. She enjoys it very much. But the paper route is a lot of work. After Diane gets the papers, she rolls them up so they will be easy to deliver. Next she puts the papers on her bicycle. Then she rides down to the sidewalk. She throws the papers carefully, so they land in front of people's doors. After Diane delivers all the papers, she hurries off to school so she won't be late.

1.  Which sentence tells the main idea of the paragraph above?
    a.  Diane throws the papers very carefully.
    b.  Diane's paper route is a lot of work.
    c.  Diane's paper route makes her late to school.
2.  Which two sentences are details that support the main idea?
    a.  Diane enjoys her paper route very much.
    b.  Diane rolls up the papers.
    c.  Diane puts the papers on her bicycle.

# Daring Kitty O'Neil

Kitty O'Neil is a very brave person. She has raced
motorcycles. And she has even been on fire! You
might have seen her on TV or at the movies. But if
you did, you wouldn't know who she was. Kitty O'Neil
is a stuntperson.

A stuntperson takes the place of an actor or an actress when there is something dangerous to do. Being a stuntperson is not a simple job. Stuntpeople must learn to do dangerous tricks. It is not easy to learn how to jump into the air on a motorcycle.

A stuntperson is bold and daring. It takes a lot of courage to do stunts. For fire stunts, Kitty is dressed in a special suit. Her whole body is protected, even her face and hair. Someone always watches to make sure nothing goes wrong. When the stunt is over, the fire will be put out.

Kitty O'Neil likes doing exciting things so much that she even has a dangerous hobby. She races cars. She has driven this special rocketlike car, called a *land vehicle,* over 320 miles an hour! This is faster than any other woman has driven.

Whether Kitty does a stunt in her work or races a car for her hobby, she first makes a careful plan to be sure everything will be done right. Many people help her too.

The picture on the left was taken shortly before Kitty broke the Woman's World Land Speed Record. In the other picture, Kitty is making a final check to make sure everyone who helps her understands what to do.

Because Kitty O'Neil is deaf, she often insists that things be written down so she knows everyone understands exactly the same directions. Kitty is bold and daring, but she's careful too.

## Think about the selection

1. Why do you think a stuntperson needs courage?
2. What does Kitty do before a stunt to make sure everything will be done right?
3. Do you think a person should do stunts without practice or help? Why do you think as you do?

## Checkpoint 3

1. Which sentence tells the main idea of "Daring Kitty O'Neil"?
   a. Kitty O'Neil has driven faster than any other woman.
   b. Kitty O'Neil has been on TV.
   c. Kitty O'Neil is bold and daring.
2. Which sentences are details that support the main idea?
   a. Kitty has a lot of courage.
   b. Kitty races motorcycles and cars.
   c. Kitty is deaf.
   d. Kitty has a dangerous hobby.

# The Surprise

Cindy heard a knock on the cellar door. "Just a minute," she called. She put down the wrench she was using to put a new lock on an old chest. She covered the chest and hurried to the door.

Cindy's friend Gene walked in. "What took you so long?" he asked.

"I'm fixing this chest as a surprise for my uncle's birthday," Cindy said. "I don't want my family to see it until it's done."

Cindy showed Gene the chest. "It looks nice," he said. "But can you stop working soon, Cindy? The baseball game starts after lunch and we need you on first base."

*4: Teach*

## Think about skills

» Most consonant letters stand for one sound. This is not so with the letters *c* and *g*. They stand for more than one sound.

Two consonant letters together usually stand for two sounds. This is not so with the letters *ll*, *ck*, *kn*, *ch*, *sh*, and *th*. Each of these pairs of letters stands for one sound. «

| | | | |
|---|---|---|---|
| lock | cellar | base | until |
| Gene | knock | nice | just |

1. In which words do you hear the sound that you hear at the beginning of *late?* Do you hear this sound at the beginning, in the middle, or at the end of the word? What letter or letters stand for this sound?
2. In which words do you hear the sound that you hear at the beginning of *soon?* Do you hear this sound at the beginning, in the middle, or at the end of the word? What letter or letters stand for this sound?
3. In which words do you hear the sound that you hear at the beginning of *jar?* What letter or letters stand for this sound?
4. In which words do you hear the sound that you hear at the beginning of *keep?* What letter or letters stand for this sound?

## Practice skills

After the baseball game, Cindy and Gene went to the drugstore to get some ice cream. They took Cindy's dog, Topper, with them.

Cindy got a giant chocolate sundae. Gene wanted a banana split. But the clerk didn't have any bananas. So Gene decided to have a pineapple shake. Before they left, they got a vanilla cone for Topper. He jumped up and ate it all.

| drugstore | chocolate | giant | game |
|-----------|-----------|--------|--------|
| clerk | lunch | Topper | jumped |

1. In which words do you hear the sound that you hear at the beginning of *get?* Do you hear this sound at the beginning, in the middle, or at the end of the word? What letter or letters stand for this sound?
2. In which words do you hear the sound that you hear at the beginning of *put?* Do you hear this sound at the beginning, in the middle, or at the end of a word? What letters stand for this sound?
3. In which words do you hear the sound that you hear at the beginning of *chase?* What letters stand for this sound?

# Noisy Nancy and Nick

by LouAnn Gaeddert

Nancy Norris lived in an apartment on the third floor of a tall building. She liked noise.

One rainy afternoon Nancy heard a noise in the hall. She ran to the door and looked out. A boy was running up and down the stairs. He was making a lot of noise. Nancy ran up the stairs after the boy. She made a lot of noise too.

"Oh, no!" called Nancy's mother. "You can't do that. You'll bother everyone in the building."

Nancy and the boy sat down on the stairs and looked at one another.

"You can't do anything in an apartment," the boy said at last. "I hate the city."

Nancy introduced herself. The boy said his name was Nick. He had just moved into an apartment on the fourth floor. He came from a small town. And so far he didn't like the city.

"Do you want to see my marigolds?" Nancy asked.

Nick nodded, and the children went to Nancy's room to look at the flowerpot on her windowsill.

"They're pretty," said Nick, "but that's not much of a garden. I grew peas, beans, and corn."

Nancy and Nick built a huge tower with Nancy's blocks. Then Nancy got her dump truck. She pushed it into the tower. The blocks crashed to the floor.

"Let's do that again," shouted Nick. They were building a new tower when they heard a bang on the floor.

"What's that?" asked Nick.

"That's the people downstairs," Nancy said. "We can't knock our tower down this time."

"I'd better go upstairs," whispered Nick. "I wish I could go back home and play with my friends. We didn't have to be quiet."

Nick turned and ran up the stairs. Nancy saw that there were tears in his eyes.

46

During dinner Nancy told her mother and father about Nick and how he had cried. "He says he hates the city," said Nancy.

"Maybe you could help him like it, "Mr. Norris said. "What do you think he'd like in the city?"

Nancy thought for a minute. "I think Nick would like the big boats. Let's go down to the docks tomorrow."

The next morning Mrs. Norris, Nancy, and Nick went down to the pier. Nancy and Nick ran up the stairs to the top deck of a huge ship. Then they ran down the stairs to the bottom deck. They were playing tag around the lifeboats when they heard a long, loud blast.

"That's the ship's whistle," Mrs. Norris said. "It means that it is time for visitors to leave."

As they walked off the ship, an officer in a white uniform said "ARRIVEDERCI" to the children. "That means 'good-by' in Italian," Mrs. Norris said. Nick and Nancy stood at the bottom of the gangplank and shouted "Arrivederci" to the people above them on the ship.

Then Mrs. Norris and the children sat on a bench. They watched the ship get ready to sail to Italy. A man came by with a cart selling pizzas. They bought their lunch from him.

"This is more fun than eating lunch in a drugstore," Nick said. "Where are we going next?"

"To the subway station," said Mrs. Norris, as they started walking down the street.

"This is a subway station," Nancy explained. She led Nick and her mother to the very end of the platform so that they could be in the first car. When the train came roaring into the station, Nancy and Nick ran to the front window. The subway started to move, and it swayed from side to side.

"What a great train!" Nick said. And he spread his feet and tried to stand without holding on.

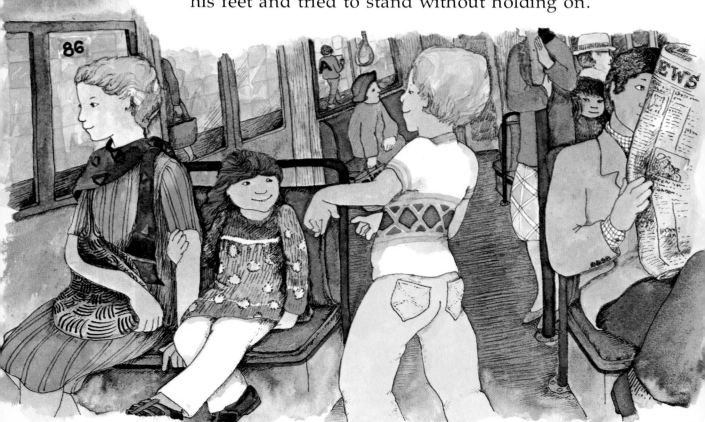

They got off at the stop nearest home and climbed the stairs to the street. Mrs. Norris said they had to stop at the butcher shop to buy meat for dinner.

The butcher greeted Nancy and her mother. He gave each child a slice of baloney. Then he cut and wrapped some meat for Mrs. Norris.

"I can't believe it," Nick said as they walked home. The city is so big, and still the store people know your name. And they even give you things. The people in our stores at home never knew my name."

"Still, small towns must be nice," said Nancy. "I'd like to live in a house where I could make a lot of noise. But there are also nice things in the city. There are . . ."

"Ocean liners, subway trains, pizza carts, and little stores," said Nick.

"And playgrounds," shouted Nancy. "Come with us tomorrow and see our swings and slides."

Nick laughed. "I'll come, but don't think you will show me anything new. Playgrounds are everywhere."

At the door of Nick's apartment, Nick thanked Nancy and her mother for the nice day.

"Arrivederci," Nick shouted as Nancy and her mother walked down the stairs to their apartment.

"Arrivederci," Nancy called back.

"Shhhh," said Mrs. Norris.

## Think about the selection

1. Put the following things from the story in the order in which they happened.
   a. Nancy and Nick rode on a subway train.
   b. Nancy met Nick.
   c. The butcher greeted Nancy by name.
   d. Nancy and Nick built a tower of blocks and then knocked it down.
   e. Nancy and Nick went to the docks to see ships.
2. Where did Nick live when he raised vegetables?
3. What two words make up each of the following?
   can't     playground     lifeboat     they're

## Checkpoint 4

| dump | huge | last | just | looked |
|------|------|------|------|--------|
| city | corn | ship | wrapped | Nick |

1. In which words above from the story do you hear the sound that you hear at the beginning of *jam?* Do you hear this sound at the beginning, in the middle, or at the end of the word? What letter or letters stand for this sound?
2. In which words do you hear the sound that you hear at the beginning of *put?* Where in each word do you hear the sound? What letter or letters stand for this sound?
3. In which words do you hear the sound that you hear at the beginning of *sat?* What letter or letters stand for this sound?
4. In which words do you hear the sound that you hear at the beginning of *can?* What letter or letters stand for this sound?

# Balloon Girl

by Rebecca Kalusky

The girl in the giant straw basket is Grace Meadows. The basket is attached to a balloon! Soon Grace's father will get in the basket. Then they'll go for a big sky ride.

Adapted and reprinted by
permission from *News Trails*,
© 1976 by Scholastic Magazines, Inc.

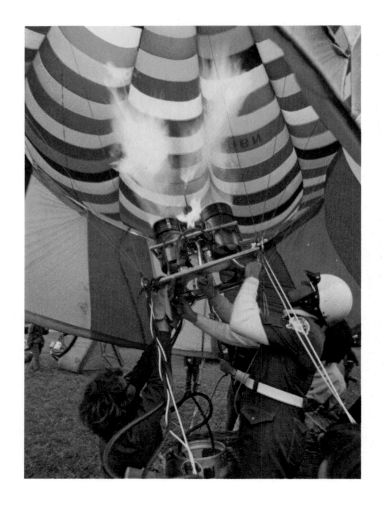

This is a burner that is under the balloon. The burner heats the air in the balloon. Hot air weighs less than unheated air. When something is lighter than unheated air, it rises. If the flame in the burner is made bigger, the balloon will rise higher. If the flame is made smaller, the balloon will go down.

Grace's father is a top balloon flyer. Sometimes he takes Grace as high as 1,000 feet in the air. That's about as far up as a 100-story building would be. Some people have gone as high as 38,000 feet. That's about where planes fly.

Up in the balloon, Grace and her dad can see around them for many miles. They fly over treetops and towns. It's so quiet up where they fly. They feel happy and free.

54

Many people enjoy the sport of ballooning. Mr. Meadows runs a balloon school and teaches people ballooning. More and more people want to learn this sport. Flyers must pass tests and get a pilot's license before they are allowed to pilot a balloon. Someday Grace hopes to be a balloon pilot. Then she will fly far and high.

## Think about the selection

1. What is ballooning?
2. Who is the "Balloon Girl"? Why do you think the story calls her that?
3. Why does Grace enjoy ballooning?
4. Why does a balloon rise?
5. Do you think you would like to go ballooning? Why or why not?

# A Glossary Is a Handy Thing

George was reading a story. He came to the
following sentence: *The iguana looked scary.*
George couldn't tell from the sentence what an
iguana is. And he didn't know how to pronounce
the word. So he looked it up in the glossary in the
back of the book. Not every book has a glossary,
but George's did. So does this book.

The words listed in a glossary are called entry
words. They are printed in heavy black type. An
entry word and everything that is said about it is
called an entry. An entry includes the definition,
or meaning, of the word. Sometimes there is also
a sentence that shows how the word can be used.

Following the entry word is the pronunciation of
the word in parentheses. The pronunciation is
given in a kind of code. Most of the signs in
the code you already know, because they're letters
of the alphabet. Look back at page 259. It explains
the code used in the Glossary of this book to show
pronunciations of words. There is also a shorter
form of the key to this code at the top of every
right-hand page in the Glossary.

When George looked up *iguana* in the glossary, the
guide words at the top of each page helped him
find the right page. The guide words tell what the
first and last entry words on a page are.

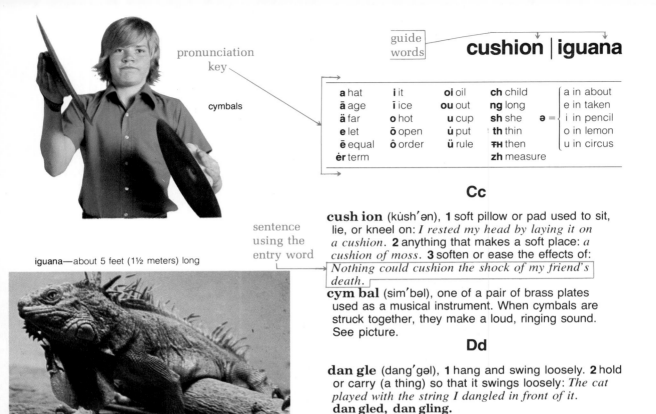

pronunciation key

cymbals

iguana—about 5 feet (1½ meters) long

| | | | | |
|---|---|---|---|---|
| **a** hat | **i** it | **oi** oil | **ch** child | a in about |
| **ā** age | **ī** ice | **ou** out | **ng** long | e in taken |
| **ä** far | **o** hot | **u** cup | **sh** she | ə = i in pencil |
| **e** let | **ō** open | **ù** put | **th** thin | o in lemon |
| **ē** equal | **ô** order | **ü** rule | **ŦH** then | u in circus |
| **ėr** term | | | **zh** measure | |

## Cc

**cush ion** (kush′ən), **1** soft pillow or pad used to sit, lie, or kneel on: *I rested my head by laying it on a cushion*. **2** anything that makes a soft place: *a cushion of moss*. **3** soften or ease the effects of: *Nothing could cushion the shock of my friend's death.*

sentence using the entry word

**cym bal** (sim′bəl), one of a pair of brass plates used as a musical instrument. When cymbals are struck together, they make a loud, ringing sound. See picture.

## Dd

**dan gle** (dang′gəl), **1** hang and swing loosely. **2** hold or carry (a thing) so that it swings loosely: *The cat played with the string I dangled in front of it.* **dan gled, dan gling.**

## Ii

entry word

**i gua na** (i gwä′nə), a large lizard with a row of spines along its back. It is found in tropical America. See picture.

pronunciation

definition

George also found that a picture of an iguana was included in the glossary.

Use the sample glossary on this page to answer these questions.

1. Is the vowel sound at the beginning of *iguana* like the vowel sound in *it* or the vowel sound in *ice?*

2. What are the guide words on this sample page?

*5: Teach*

3. What entry word would you look up to find the meaning of *dangling*?
4. Which definition of *cushion* tells what the word means in the following sentence?
   When Sarita's bike hit a bump, the grass cushioned her fall.
5. Besides the definition, what else in the Glossary helps you understand the meaning of *cymbal*?

## Practice skills

Use the Glossary in the back of this book to answer these questions.

1. Look up the entry word *aisle*. What are the guide words on that page? Could the entry word *aquarium* be found on that page? Why or why not?
2. Find the pronunciation of the entry word *molasses*. Is the first vowel sound like the first vowel sound in *about* or the first vowel sound in *open*?
3. Find the entry for *dash*. Which definition tells what *dash* means in the following sentence?
   Tamiko put a dash of ginger in the pudding.
4. Besides the definition, what else in the Glossary helps you understand the meaning of *dolphin*?
5. What entry word would you look up to find the meaning of *dared*?
6. Find the pronunciation of the entry word *stirrup*. Is the first vowel sound like the one in *it* or the vowel sound in *term*? Is the second vowel sound like the second vowel sound in *circus* or the vowel sound in *cup*?

# What Is a Pig?

by Robin Lesser

Every pig has a strong snout. It helps a pig root, or dig, for food. And pigs have barrel-shaped bodies and short legs. Yet they can swim well and run quickly. In fact, pigs can run as fast as most people!

People sometimes call pigs names. They say pigs are greedy and dirty. But these names are not fair. It is true that pigs eat almost anything. They eat roots, berries, insects, eggs, and many other things. But most wild pigs never eat too much. And pigs are not dirty. They like mud baths, but so do elephants. Mud soothes insect bites. It also protects and cools a pig's hide.

From "What Makes a Pig a Pig" by Robin Lesser. Reprinted from *Ranger Rick's Nature Magazine,* March 1976, by permission of the publisher, National Wildlife Federation.

peccary

Hampshire sow and piglets

There are many different kinds of pigs. Some are raised for meat or leather. Others have tusks, a mane, whiskers, or warts. And some even have babies with stripes!

Pigs can't see well. But they can hear and smell very well. Pigs are also very smart. Bush pigs, which live in Africa, have good memories. If a bush pig finds a trap, it will stay away from that spot for weeks.

Wild boars are the giants among wild pigs. They can weigh as much as a lion! They live mostly in Europe and Asia. And they build their own sunshades! They cut grass with their tusks. Then they spread this grass out like a blanket. They crawl under this blanket of grass, raising it until it catches on the taller uncut grass which holds the sunshade up. This shields the pigs from the hot sun.

## Think about the selection

1. How does a pig use its snout to get food?
2. Does a pig see well? hear well? have a good sense of smell?
3. Do you think pigs are smart? Explain why you think as you do.
4. What other animal besides the pig likes to take mud baths? How do mud baths help them?
5. Why does the author think bush pigs have good memories?
6. Why do people raise pigs?
7. When a wild boar makes a sunshade, what holds the sunshade up?

## Checkpoint 5

Use the Glossary to answer these questions.

1. What entry word would you look up to find the meaning of *soothes*?
2. Find the pronunciation of the entry word *peccary*. Is the first vowel sound in *peccary* like the vowel sound in *let* or like the first vowel sound in *equal*? Is the second vowel sound in *peccary* like the vowel sound in *age* or the second vowel sound in *taken*?
3. Which definition of *greedy* tells what the word means in the following sentence?
   The greedy child ate ten pancakes in five minutes.
4. Besides the definitions, what else in the entry for *greedy* helped you understand the meaning of the first definition?
5. What are the guide words on page 270?

# Freckle Power

Jill saw red every time she was teased about her freckles. Her grandmother said, "You're as pretty as a picture with those freckles." But Jill thought they were ugly as mud.

Jill decided to start a club for people with freckles. She asked her friend Rick to join.

"I don't want to be in a club that's only for people with freckles," Rick said.

Jill's face fell when Rick said no.

## Think about skills

The story says that Jill saw red. That doesn't mean that she really did see red. It means that Jill was angry. The phrase *saw red* is a figure of speech. Figures of speech use words differently from their usual meanings. They make reading more interesting.

1. Did Jill's face really fall?

64

How would you describe a person who moves slowly? You might say the person is as slow as a turtle or as slow as molasses. These figures of speech are more interesting than just saying someone moves slowly.

2.  What figure of speech did Jill use to describe her freckles?

You know that pronouns are words that stand for the names of people, animals, and things. In the first sentence of the story you figured out that *she* stood for *Jill.*

3.  In the sentences below, what does each underlined pronoun stand for?
4.  What is the figure of speech in each sentence?
5.  What do you think each figure of speech means?

A.  Debbie looked down <u>her</u> nose at the idea.
B.  Tom was so sad that <u>his</u> chin was dragging.

## Practice skills

1.  In the sentences below, what does each underlined pronoun stand for?
2.  What is the figure of speech in each sentence?
3.  What do you think each figure of speech means?

A.  Kim was so happy that <u>her</u> face lit up.
B.  The boys don't see eye to eye on <u>their</u> problem.
C.  When Fred left, <u>he</u> was as quiet as a mouse.

# Pig Disappears

by Robert Fremlin

Squirrel hurried along the road to Pig's pen.

"What can be wrong now?" he worried. "I knew something would happen. If it isn't one trouble, it's another."

Cat was waiting in front of Pig's pen. Cat looked cross.

"Cat!" shouted Squirrel. "I got your message and came as fast as I could. What is the matter?"

"Pfah," said Cat. "Pig is the matter. Look."

Cat pointed to a sign on Pig's door.

"What! Pig selling his pen? Why would Pig do such a thing?" asked Squirrel.

Cat frowned. "Pig has run away. He left this note in my mailbox, and I've just come to see if it's true."

*6: Apply*

"Oh, Cat, this is terrible news," said Squirrel.

"It's not very good poetry either," said Cat, looking at the note.

Suddenly there was a crash from inside Pig's pen. Squirrel jumped behind Cat.

"I think we had better see what that noise is all about," whispered Cat. "Come on, Squirrel."

They pushed open the door and went inside. They found Pig in the kitchen, stuffing food into a suitcase on the floor.

"Oh!" said Cat. "In the kitchen. I might have known."

"Not for long," said Pig. "I'm on my way as soon as I finish packing. Squirrel, will you hand me that big bag of candy?"

"But why are you running away?" asked Squirrel.

"Because nobody wants a pig around, that's why," said Pig. "Yesterday at the picnic everyone was mad at me because I ate all the cake. And Rabbit won't let me come to dinner again just because I helped myself to all the lettuce and fell into the pie. And even you, Cat, said I have bad manners."

"I did *not* say that," said Cat. "I said that you eat like a pig."

"Oh, it's no use," said Pig. "I'm going. Can you reach that big jar of pickles, Cat?"

Pig, Cat, and Squirrel crowded around the suitcase.

"Let me see," said Pig. "I've got the catsup, candy bars . . ."

"There are no clothes in that suitcase," said Cat.

". . . peanut butter, jelly," counted Pig.

"But Pig, we don't *want* you to run away," said Squirrel.

"I'm almost gone," said Pig. "Almost out the door, in fact."

"What is in that big bag on the table?" asked Cat.

"My lunch, of course," said Pig.

"Pfah," said Cat.

Pig tried to shut the suitcase. It would not close. He stood on it. It still would not close.

"Cat, Squirrel, will you help me?" Pig asked.

Pig, Cat and Squirrel stood on the suitcase. They jumped on it. They danced on it. But it would not close.

"It must be broken," said Pig.

"It must be that big jar of pickles," said Cat.

"Good!" said Squirrel. "If you cannot close your suitcase, you cannot run away."

"Well," said Cat. "If you take something out, you can close it."

"But I cannot take out the food," said Pig.

They looked at the suitcase on the floor. Catsup was leaking out the side.

"Poor me," groaned Pig. "I thought if I ran away I could be different. Now I feel terrible."

"But Pig," said Squirrel, "we like you just as you are."

*6: Apply*

"Besides, there's really nothing wrong with being a pig," said Cat.

Pig looked at his two friends. "I suppose if I *must* be a pig I would rather be a pig here than anywhere else," he sighed.

"Then you'll stay?" asked Squirrel. "Good! Why don't we unpack everything and have a party?"

"A not-going-away party," said Cat.

"Well, I *am* a bit hungry," said Pig.

So they emptied Pig's suitcase on the kitchen table. Then they all had a fine dinner.

## Think about the selection

1. What made Pig feel unhappy at the beginning of the story?
2. Do you think the things everyone said about pigs were fair? Why or why not?
3. Why did Pig decide not to run away?

## Checkpoint 6

1. In the sentences below, what does each underlined pronoun stand for?
2. What is the figure of speech in each sentence?
3. What do you think each figure of speech means?

A. Pig said that <u>he</u> didn't care a fig.
B. "No, Pig, <u>I</u> only said that <u>you</u> eat like a pig," Cat explained.

74

# Is It Fact or Fiction?

"Hey, Bob!" Sue called to her brother. "Let me read you something from each of these books. You tell me whether what I read is fact or fiction."

Bob looked up from his book. "How can I tell?" he asked. "I don't know one from the other."

"Sure you do!" Sue said. "If it tells something that's known to be true, then it's fact. Facts are things that are known to have happened. But fiction is made up or imagined. So if it's a story that is not fact, then you know it's fiction. Do you see how they are different?" Sue asked.

"Now I do," Bob answered. "Read away!"

Sue picked up a book. As she opened it to read, Bob said, "Wait a minute. If you read something that sounds true, how will I know if it really is fact?"

"That's a good point," Sue said. "If it sounds like something that can be proved, then you know it's probably fact. And if it sounds like something made up, you know it's fiction. Now listen to this paragraph."

It was a bad day. The fog was so thick that we had to cut it with a knife. Then we rolled it back and stepped through it.

"That's easy," said Bob. "That couldn't happen, so it's fiction. Read another paragraph."

Sue picked up another book and began to read.

The largest city in the United States is New York. It has more than 7,000,000 people. The United Nations Building is in New York.

"That sounds true," said Bob. "So it's probably fact."

Now see if you can tell the difference between fact and fiction. Look at "What Is a Pig?" pages 60–62, and "Pig Disappears," pages 66–73. Then answer the following questions.

1. Which story is probably fact? How do you know?
2. Which story is fiction? How do you know?
3. What is fiction? What is fact?

## Practice skills

1. Which paragraph below is probably fact? How do you know?
2. Which paragraph below is fiction? How do you know?

A. **There are many different kinds of spiders in the United States. And spiders live in many different places. Some live in trees. Some live in fields. And others live in water.**
B. **Joey was the only nine-year-old boy who had wings and could fly. He had been able to fly since he was six. And now Joey's wings were very strong.**

# Big SNOW in Buffalo

7: Apply

In January, 1977, there was a snowstorm in the city of Buffalo, New York. It was the most snow Buffalo had ever had. More than twelve feet of snow fell.

The snow that fell in Buffalo caused schools and businesses to close. Snow blocked doorways and streets and no one could go anywhere. Trains stopped running because there was too much snow on the tracks. The airport closed because the planes couldn't take off or land. People who were at school or work when the storm began had to stay in firehouses, police stations, and schools. They couldn't get home because of the snow.

Many people couldn't go out to get food and medicine, so those who had sleds and snowmobiles helped. They delivered groceries and medicine to people who couldn't get around. Snowmobiles and sleds were more useful than cars in Buffalo.

After the snow stopped falling, people began the job of digging out. It wasn't easy, but slowly the snow was cleared away.

## Think about the selection

1. Where did this snowstorm take place?
2. Why did the trains stop running?
3. What were some other things that happened because of the snowstorm?
4. Why do you think snowmobiles and sleds were more useful than cars in Buffalo?

## Checkpoint 7

1. Is "Big Snow in Buffalo" fact or fiction? How do you know?

Bonus
Selection

# FIREFLY SONG

Flickering firefly
             give me light
             light
once more before I sleep

Dancing firefly
             wandering firefly
             light
once more before I sleep

White light sailing
                white light winking
just once more before I sleep

—Ojibwa

Adapted from Henry R. Schoolcraft, *Historical and
Statistical Information, Respecting the History, Condition,
and Prospects of the Indian Tribes of the United States,*
Philadelphia, 1851–57.

# What Is the Sound?

<u>These</u> are not <u>ferns</u>.
These are <u>weeds</u>.
Weeds make <u>me</u> sneeze.
<u>Please</u> take <u>them</u> away.

The <u>bus</u> can't get
<u>up</u> to the <u>curb</u>. A <u>huge</u>
<u>blue</u> <u>truck</u> is in the
way.

## Think about skills

A numbered sentence below explains which vowel sound you would usually expect in each underlined word.

1. One vowel letter in a word followed by one or more consonant letters usually stands for a short vowel sound: *them, bus, up, truck.*
2. This is not so if the consonant after the vowel is r. Then the vowel sound is r-controlled: *ferns, curb.*
3. A vowel letter in a word followed by one or more consonants and a final *e* usually stands for a long vowel sound: *these, huge.*
4. Two vowel letters together in a word usually stand for the long sound of the first vowel: *weeds, sneeze, please, blue.*
5. One vowel letter at the end of a word usually stands for a long vowel sound: *me.*

Read each paragraph at the left. Look at the words at the right. Tell what vowel sound you hear in each word and why you expect to hear that sound.

The man would like to make his car gray. He can paint it.

man   car   make   gray
can                        paint

The puppy got my new doll. So now her dress is torn. She has a hole in the toe of her sock. She looks like an old doll.

got   torn   hole   toe   so
doll
sock

Last night we had a picnic. One child dropped his pie and ice cream in the dirt. Then he began to cry.

his   dirt   ice   pie   cry
in

Do the words *old, night,* and *child* have one vowel letter followed by one or more consonant letters? Do they have short vowel sounds? No, they do not. These words have long vowel sounds.

## Practice skills
How are the words in each row alike?

1. fish          top          sat          cup

2. leaf          pie          road          glue

3. cart          jerk          fork          stir

4. these          mule          plate          time

5. colt          right          bolt          wild

6. fly          no          she          by

# LOST AND FOUND

by Fain Matthews Williams

Mrs. Lopez had just moved into a new neighborhood. She wanted to make friends with her neighbors, but she didn't know how. She was too shy.

Then one day Mrs. Lopez began to find things. She was out taking a walk when she found a skate key. "Look at this!" she said to herself. "But what am I going to do with it? I guess I'll just take it home. I'll find out who it belongs to some other day."

8: Apply

The next day she found a red hat. "I'll just put this with the skate key," she said. After that she began to carry her shopping bag with her on her walks.

Soon the shopping bag was almost full. Mrs. Lopez began to worry. She knew that she must find out who owned all the lost things. But she was too shy to ask anyone.

When she found a puppy, she knew she had to do something. "After all," she said, "I can keep a key and a hat in a shopping bag, but not a puppy!"

So Mrs. Lopez went home to think. She sat in her rocking chair and thought and thought. Suddenly she jumped up. "That's it!" she cried. "I know just what to do!"

What a busy day Mrs. Lopez had! She moved some furniture. Then she pounded in some nails.

Early the next morning the children came out to play. And the fathers and mothers came out to go to work. They all were surprised to see the sign on Mrs. Lopez's fence.

LOST THINGS CAN BE FOUND HERE.

PLEASE RING BELL.

Mrs. Lopez didn't have long to wait before the bell rang. She opened the door and saw a boy.

"Hi!" he said with a smile. "Do you really find lost things?"

Mrs. Lopez smiled back and said, "Why, yes I do. You must have lost something. Come on in. We'll see if I have it."

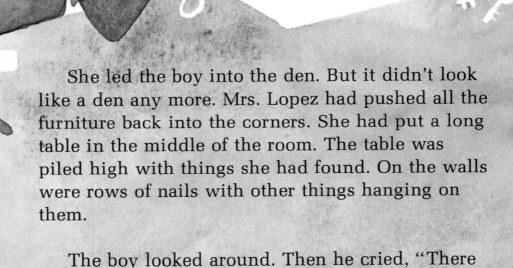

She led the boy into the den. But it didn't look like a den any more. Mrs. Lopez had pushed all the furniture back into the corners. She had put a long table in the middle of the room. The table was piled high with things she had found. On the walls were rows of nails with other things hanging on them.

The boy looked around. Then he cried, "There it is! My skate key!" He turned to Mrs. Lopez and grinned. "Why, you really do find things!"

Before the boy could thank her and leave, the bell rang again. All day long Mrs. Lopez was running back and forth, letting people look for their lost things. It was a happy day for her. One of the best parts was seeing the look in the eyes of the girl when she picked up her lost puppy. Mrs. Lopez was so busy that she forgot to be shy. She was laughing and talking with all the rest.

The next morning Mrs. Lopez went into the den. She stopped in surprise. "Everything is gone!" she said. "And I haven't had time to find any new things." She was sad as she thought of how quiet her house would be again.

Just then the bell rang. Mrs. Lopez opened the door. There stood the girl who had lost the puppy. "Hi!" she said. "I brought my puppy over to play with you."

Right behind the girl was one of the fathers with a fresh apple pie. And right behind him was one of the mothers. "I noticed that your gate was loose," she said. "So I'll fix it for you."

Then Mrs. Lopez knew that she had been wrong. She *had* found something new, after all. She had found some friends.

8: Apply

# Think about the selection

1. What was the problem in this story?
2. How was the problem solved?
3. Why was it hard for Mrs. Lopez to make friends in her new neighborhood?
4. Why didn't Mrs. Lopez feel shy when the people came to get their lost things?

## Checkpoint 8

How are the words in each of these rows alike?

1. red      fresh     thank     not
2. shy      she       go        he
3. skate    home      smile     gate
4. nails    see       wait      leave
5. forth    her       parts     girl

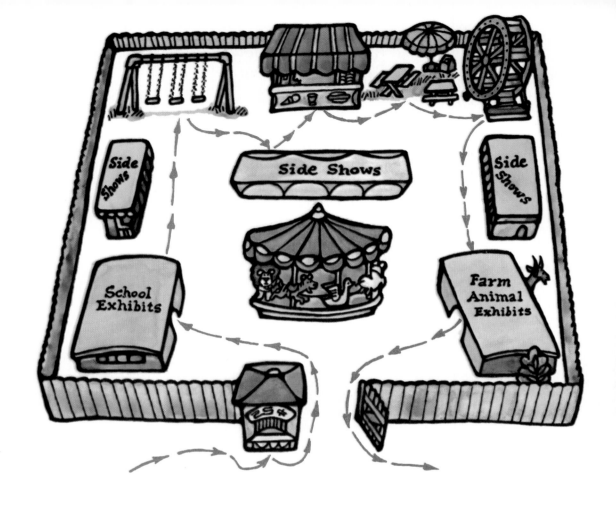

# A Trip to the Farm Fair

Pam and Yetta went to the farm fair. The picture map above shows the fairgrounds. The line with arrows shows where the two girls went at the fair.

Look at the picture map. Find the ticket booth outside the fence of the fairgrounds. That's where Pam and Yetta started. After they bought their tickets, the girls went first to the school exhibits. Those exhibits were closer to the gate than the swings were.

94

Follow the arrows on the picture map. You will see that after Pam and Yetta went to the school exhibits, they went to the swings.

1. Where did the girls go after they went to the swings?
2. Which was closer to the main gate, the swings or the merry-go-round?

## Practice skills

Use the picture map to answer these questions.

1. Pam and Yetta sat down at a picnic table. Where were they just before that?
2. Where did they go after they left the picnic table?
3. What was the last place the girls visited at the fair?
4. The girls did not go on one of the rides. Which one?

# A Visit to a Zoo in Winter

Where winters are very cold, many animals in zoos stay inside. But some animals whose natural homes are in cold parts of the world are outside. These animals have thick fur and a good layer of fat beneath the skin to help them survive the cold.

Some tigers live only where it's warm. But this is a Siberian tiger. Siberian tigers come from cold pine forests. In winter their fur is very long and thick. These tigers are larger than the kinds of tigers that live in warmer places. They need more food in cold weather.

Some bears go into a deep sleep in the coldest weather. But some polar bears are outside in winter. They can even take a swim in very cold water. The water doesn't mat their fur. So the bears stay warm, even when their fur is wet.

Wolves stay outside in winter. During very cold weather, their fur gets fluffy. Air is held in among the hairs and helps the wolves stay warm.

Snowy owls are out in winter. They live on mice and other small animals. In a bad winter, the snowy owls' food gets hard to find. Then the birds fly farther south. Sometimes a snowy owl is seen in a city park.

Arctic foxes can stand the coldest weather even better than polar bears can. These foxes are mostly gray and brown in summer. In late summer they begin to change color. Their fur is white in winter to match the snow. This color change protects wild Arctic foxes, because other animals cannot see them very well.

Dall sheep are the only wild white sheep in the world. In winter their coats are very thick. Their hoofs are made for climbing in slippery places.

Reindeer are well protected from the cold. They have thick coats of hair. Each hair is hollow and is full of air. A reindeer's wide hoofs keep it from sinking into the snow.

Walruses come from the sea near the North Pole. They climb out onto big pieces of floating ice. They are used to very cold weather. Under a walrus's skin is a layer of fat which may be several inches thick. This fat protects the animal's body from the chill of the icy waters. Walruses are outside when you visit the zoo in winter.

Yaks belong to the cow family. Their hair is long and shaggy. Their natural home is in very high mountains. Yaks really like the cold. They can't stand hot weather.

**Think about the selection**

1. Is "A Visit to a Zoo in Winter" fact or fiction? Why do you think so?

2. Which one of the following sentences tells the main idea of "A Visit to a Zoo in Winter"? Which sentences are details that support that main idea?

   a. Siberian tigers have very long, thick hair in winter.

   b. The fur of Arctic foxes changes from gray or brown to white to match the winter snow.

   c. A walrus has a thick layer of fat under the skin to protect its body from the chill of icy waters.

   d. Many kinds of animals can stay outside in cold winter weather.

*9: Apply*

# Checkpoint 9

The picture map below shows a zoo. The line with the arrows shows the route the Nudd family used to see the animals during the winter. Use the map to answer the questions below.

1.  The Nudd family entered the zoo at the south gate. What animals did they go to see first? second? third?
2.  What animals did the Nudds stop to see right after they visited the Arctic foxes?
3.  Where did the Nudds go right after they saw the snowy owls?
4.  The Nudds did not see all the animals in the zoo. Which animals didn't they see?
5.  What gate did the Nudds use to leave the zoo?

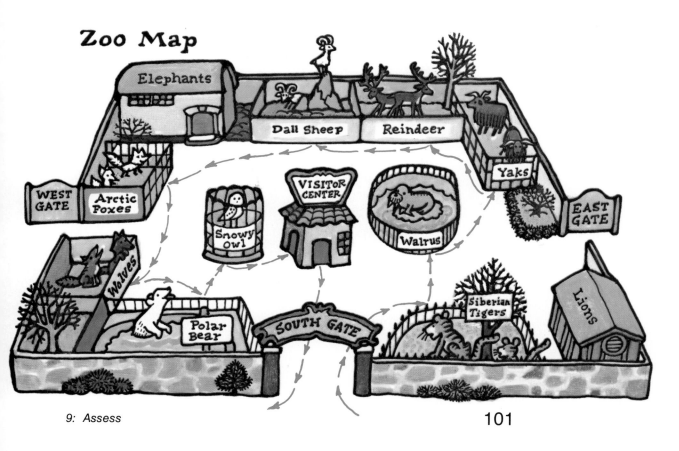

Zoo Map

# TOO BIG, Too Little

by Ann Louis

Tommy took big steps to keep up with his mother and his older brother, Edward. His little brother, David, rode in the stroller. They were in a big department store.

"May I go upstairs to look at bicycles?" asked Edward.

"Yes," said his mother. "Meet us in the toy department."

"May I go too?" asked Tommy.

Adapted from *Children's Playmate* magazine, copyright © 1973 by The Saturday Evening Post Company, Indianapolis, Indiana.

"No," said Edward, "you're too little." Edward went up the escalator.

"Too little," grumbled Tommy.

"This aisle is too crowded for the stroller," Mother said to Tommy. "Please stay with it for a minute."

Tommy held the handle of the stroller. He said to himself, "Too little to go with Edward. Big enough to stay with David."

When Mother came back, they all went upstairs. They took the elevator. A very big man rode up with them. Tommy had to move very close to his mother to make room for the very big man.

"I wonder if he's too big to ride the escalator," thought Tommy.

At the toy department a very small woman asked, "May I help you?"

"Yes," said Mother. "I'd like to see a bouncing horse, please."

"This way, please," said the very small woman.

"I wonder if she's too little to sell anything but toys," thought Tommy.

"Let your son try this horse," said the woman.

Mother put David on the bouncing horse.

"I want to try it too," said Tommy.

"Oh, no," said the woman. "You're too big."

"I see," said Tommy, "too big."

Edward came back from the bicycle department.

"We have to go now," said Mother, "or we'll miss the bus." They left the store and got on the bus.

Tommy watched other people get on the bus. Soon all the seats were full. Some people had to stand. A boy and a girl got on the bus. She was tall enough to reach the strap hanging from the ceiling. He was short enough to hold onto the pole below the other people's hands.

Everyone seemed to be just the right size for something. "I bet no one else is my size," thought Tommy. "I'm either too big or too little for everything."

"Here's our stop," said Mother.

Tommy, his mother, Edward, and David got off at the corner. Mother looked in her purse. Then she looked in her pockets.

"Oh, no!" she said. "I left the key on the hook in the kitchen."

"Could we get in the little kitchen window?" asked Tommy.

"Let's try," said Mother.

Edward took off the screen. He opened the tiny window and tried to crawl inside. He couldn't do it. "I'm too big," said Edward.

"I can get inside," said Tommy. "I'm not too big to squeeze in the window, and I'm not too little to reach the key. I'm just the right size."

And he was.

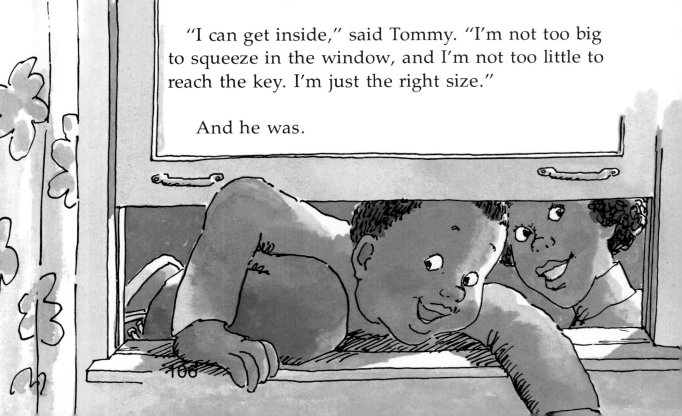

## Think about the selection

1. In "Too Big, Too Little," who was taller—Tommy or Edward? How do you know?
2. What was the problem in "Too Big, Too Little"? How was it solved?
3. Which of the following tells what happened first? next? last?
   a. Tommy's mother found out that she had left the key inside the house.
   b. Tommy and his family went home on the bus.
   c. Tommy crawled through the window to get the key.
4. How did Tommy feel when he couldn't go upstairs with Edward? How did Tommy feel when he saw the people on the bus? Why do you answer as you do?
5. How do you think Tommy felt after he crawled through the window to get the key? Why do you think as you do?

# Section One Checkpoint

## Word Identification Tests

### Subtest 1

1. In which word do you hear the sound that you hear at the beginning of <u>cold</u>?
   ⓐ cent    ⓑ neck    ⓒ lost    ⓓ DK

2. In what part of the word did you hear it?
   ⓐ beginning    ⓑ middle    ⓒ end    ⓓ DK

3. In which word do you hear the sound that you hear at the beginning of <u>just</u>?
   ⓐ pages    ⓑ finger    ⓒ grow    ⓓ DK

4. In what part of the word did you hear it?
   ⓐ beginning    ⓑ middle    ⓒ end    ⓓ DK

5. In which word do you hear the sound that you hear at the beginning of <u>chair</u>?
   ⓐ clock    ⓑ shine    ⓒ reach    ⓓ DK

6. In what part of the word did you hear it?
   ⓐ beginning    ⓑ middle    ⓒ end    ⓓ DK

7. In which word do you hear the sound that you hear at the beginning of <u>soap</u>?
   ⓐ cutting    ⓑ lettuce    ⓒ pocket    ⓓ DK

8. In what part of the word did you hear it?
   ⓐ beginning    ⓑ middle    ⓒ end    ⓓ DK

## Subtest 2

*What vowel sound do you hear in the underlined word?*

9. Susan dropped her <u>fork</u>.
   ⓐ short    ⓑ long    ⓒ r-controlled    ⓓ DK

10. Tommy had picked a <u>bunch</u> of flowers.
    ⓐ short    ⓑ long    ⓒ r-controlled    ⓓ DK

11. It was getting dark, <u>so</u> Bill went home.
    ⓐ short    ⓑ long    ⓒ r-controlled    ⓓ DK

12. Joe and Anita have a new <u>sled</u>.
    ⓐ short    ⓑ long    ⓒ r-controlled    ⓓ DK

13. Do you know how to <u>make</u> ice cream?
    ⓐ short    ⓑ long    ⓒ r-controlled    ⓓ DK

14. The <u>north</u> wind was very cold.
    ⓐ short    ⓑ long    ⓒ r-controlled    ⓓ DK

15. Terry likes to read <u>true</u> stories.
    ⓐ short    ⓑ long    ⓒ r-controlled    ⓓ DK

16. Ann likes to <u>feed</u> the birds.
    ⓐ short    ⓑ long    ⓒ r-controlled    ⓓ DK

17. My aunt and uncle live on a <u>farm</u>.
    ⓐ short    ⓑ long    ⓒ r-controlled    ⓓ DK

Possible Word Identification Score: 17

# Comprehension Tests

## Subtest 3
*What does the underlined word in each sentence stand for?*

1. Before Jim left, the cook fixed a sandwich for <u>him</u>.
   - ⓐ the cook
   - ⓑ the sandwich
   - ⓒ Jim
   - ⓓ DK

2. Sue and Jo were ten minutes late, so <u>they</u> missed the play.
   - ⓐ Sue and Jo
   - ⓑ the play
   - ⓒ ten minutes
   - ⓓ DK

## Subtest 4
*What does the underlined part of each sentence mean?*

3. Joe knew he'd <u>be in hot water</u> if he didn't get the job done.
   - ⓐ get a prize
   - ⓑ have trouble
   - ⓒ take a bath
   - ⓓ DK

4. When Mary started to complain, Sally told her to <u>hold her tongue</u>.
   - ⓐ touch her mouth
   - ⓑ talk more slowly
   - ⓒ stop talking
   - ⓓ DK

## Subtest 5
*Which meaning best fits the underlined word in the sentence?*

5. The <u>point</u> of the pin was bent.
   - ⓐ place
   - ⓑ sharp end
   - ⓒ aim
   - ⓓ DK

6. The train <u>leaves</u> at noon.
   - ⓐ goes away
   - ⓑ let alone
   - ⓒ more than one leaf
   - ⓓ DK

7. She leaned on her <u>cane</u>.
   - ⓐ stick used in walking
   - ⓑ plant with a jointed stem
   - ⓒ beat with a stick
   - ⓓ DK

8. Pull your <u>cap</u> over your ears.
   - ⓐ highest part
   - ⓑ covering for the head
   - ⓒ bottle top
   - ⓓ DK

9. Help me put the new sheets on the <u>bed</u> in my room.
   - ⓐ something to sleep on
   - ⓑ place to plant flowers
   - ⓒ put in the ground
   - ⓓ DK

## Subtest 6

*Read the story and then answer the questions.*

David wanted a light for his new bicycle. He did a lot of things to earn the money he needed. He raked leaves for Mr. Hill. He stayed with the baby while Mrs. King went to the store for milk. Mr. Ling paid him to help clean the garage. He helped a neighbor wash her car. Finally he had enough money for the light.

10. Which sentence tells the main idea of the paragraph?
    ⓐ David helped a neighbor wash her car.
    ⓑ David earned money to buy a light for his bicycle.
    ⓒ David raked leaves for Mr. Hill.

11. Which sentence is a detail that supports the main idea?
    ⓐ David has a new bicycle.
    ⓑ Mrs. King went to the store to get some milk.
    ⓒ Mr. Ling paid David to help clean the garage.

## Subtest 7

*Read each paragraph and decide whether it is fact or fiction.*

12. A rabbit is a furry animal with long ears and a short fluffy tail. Rabbits don't walk or run. They move about by hopping on their back legs. Rabbits live in many parts of the world.
    ⓐ fact    ⓑ fiction    ⓒ DK

13. The girl got on her horse, Charger, and galloped to the top of a high hill. Then she said three words to it, and it went flying into the clouds. The horse and rider were soon in space. They were going to the moon.
    ⓐ fact    ⓑ fiction    ⓒ DK

14. Ed wanted to go swimming. But Jeff wanted to go to the ball game. They talked it over. Then Ed said, "We'll go to the ball game today. Then next week we'll go swimming."
    ⓐ fact    ⓑ fiction    ⓒ DK

# Study and Research Test

## Subtest 8

*Use page 270 in your book to answer these questions.*

1. What are the guide words on this page?
   - ⓐ *sharp* and *shield*
   - ⓑ *sharp* and *snout*
   - ⓒ *slide* and *snout*
   - ⓓ DK

2. Which of these could be an entry word on this page?
   - ⓐ sift
   - ⓑ stalk
   - ⓒ salute
   - ⓓ DK

3. Look at the pronunciation of the entry for *sharp.* Which key word has the same vowel sound as *sharp?*
   - ⓐ age
   - ⓑ far
   - ⓒ hat
   - ⓓ DK

4. Find the entry for *sniff.* Which definition tells what *sniff* means in the following sentence?
   The bear sniffed at the old tire by the roadside.
   - ⓐ 1
   - ⓑ 2
   - ⓒ 3
   - ⓓ DK

5. What entry word would you look up to find the meaning of *silencing?*
   - ⓐ silenced
   - ⓑ silent
   - ⓒ silence
   - ⓓ DK

6. Which definition of *silent* is shown in the picture?
   - ⓐ 1
   - ⓑ 2
   - ⓒ 3
   - ⓓ 4

7. Which key word has the same vowel sound as the first vowel sound in *silent?*
   - ⓐ it
   - ⓑ taken
   - ⓒ ice
   - ⓓ DK

112

# The Hare and the Hedgehog

One bright, sunny morning a hedgehog was sitting at the door of her home.

Suddenly she decided that a walk before breakfast might be good for her. So off she went. She had not gone far when she saw a hare under a berry bush.

From *More Friends Old and New.* Scott, Foresman and Company, 1965.        113

"Good morning, Neighbor Hare," the friendly hedgehog called.

The hare seemed very surprised to see the hedgehog. "Why are you out so early?" asked the hare.

"I want to find out how my turnips are growing," answered the hedgehog. "I'm taking a walk to the turnip field."

The hare gave a loud laugh. "Taking a walk!" he said. "It must be very hard to walk on legs as short as yours."

That made the hedgehog very angry. "I suppose
you think long legs are much better than short
ones," she said. "Well, let's find out. Let's run a
race in the turnip field to see if they are."

"Very well," said the hare with a grin. "No sooner
said than done."

And the hare started off to the field.

"Wait!" called the hedgehog. "I want to eat
breakfast first. I'll meet you at the turnip field in a
few minutes."

Then away went the hedgehog as fast as her short
legs could carry her.

When the hedgehog reached home, she asked her cousin to go to the turnip field with her. On the way she told him about the race.

Then she said, "You can help me play a joke on the hare. He will run up the first row of turnips. I will start up the second row. You can hide at the top of my row and wait. When the hare gets to the top of his row, you jump out and say, 'I'm here first!'"

Soon the hedgehog and her cousin came to the turnip field. She went at once to the bottom of the second row. Her cousin ran to hide at the top of the same row.

The hedgehog waited until the hare got to the bottom of the first row. Then she said, "Let's start."

"Fine," said the hare. "Ready! Go!" And away he
ran with all his might.

But the hedgehog took only two steps. Then she
stopped still and waited under the cool turnip
leaves.

Just before the hare got to the top of his row, a
hedgehog popped out. "I'm here first!" said the
hedgehog.

117

"Well, well!" said the surprised hare. "This is very strange. Let's race back to the bottom of our rows."

He turned and dashed down his row as fast as the wind. But before he reached the bottom of the row, he saw a hedgehog pop out.

"I'm here first!" said the hedgehog.

This time the hare was more angry than surprised. "We must race again!" he shouted.

The hedgehog laughed to herself over the joke she and her cousin were playing. "No sooner said than done!" she cried. "Ready! Go!"

The hare went leaping up his row. But just before he reached the top, the hedgehog's cousin popped up his head.

He called out, "I'm here first again! You act very tired, Neighbor Hare."

The angry hare did not even answer. He just ran to the bottom of the row.

Up and down his row dashed the hare. Each time, one hedgehog or the other popped out and said, "I'm here first!"

Finally the hare gave up. He was too tired to race any more. Without saying a word, he hopped slowly off to his home in the bushes.

The hedgehogs stayed in the field and ate turnips until they were full. Both of them wondered if the angry hare would ever boast about his long legs again.

# Section Two

# How Can You Tell?

Kate went into her room. She stood on a stool to put books on a high shelf.

Ray took a bus to town. He saw a show about a clown and a pet crow.

## Think about skills

When you see a word with the letters *oo* or *ow*, you may have to read a whole sentence to decide what vowel sound the word has.

1. Which underlined words in the first paragraph have the same vowel sound?
2. Which underlined words in the second paragraph have the same vowel sound?

## Practice skills

Which underlined words in each sentence have the same vowel sound?

1. The food Tim took to the picnic was good.
2. The cook at school hurt her foot.
3. Do you know how to grow green beans?
4. The owl painted on my bowl is brown.

122

# Jack and the Beanstalk

Once upon a time there lived a woman who had
a son named Jack. The woman and her son were
very poor. All they had was a small house and
a cow.

Jack and his mother worked hard in their garden
to grow food. But they never had enough to eat.

Jack's mother needed money to buy food and
warm clothes. She told Jack to take their cow to
town and sell it. So Jack started to town with
the cow.

On the way Jack met a man. The man said, "Good morning. Where are you going this fine day?"

"To town to sell the cow," Jack answered.

The man said, "I'll trade you some magic beans for your cow." The man held out his hand. He showed Jack some beans of many bright colors.

The colors of the beans seemed to grow brighter as Jack looked at them. Jack wanted the beans a lot. So he gave away the cow and took the beans home.

When Jack's mother saw the beans she was very angry. She threw the beans out the window. Then she sent Jack to bed without his supper.

The next morning Jack saw something growing outside his window. The magic beans had grown into a huge beanstalk! It was so tall that Jack could not see the top of it.

Jack went out and started to climb the beanstalk. He climbed and climbed until he got to the top. And there, in front of him, Jack saw a strange new land.

Jack started walking. Soon he came to a castle and knocked on the door. A woman opened the door.

"I'm hungry," said Jack. "May I have some bread?"

"Yes," said the woman. "But you must eat quickly. My husband is a mean giant. If he comes home and finds you, he'll eat you for dinner."

While Jack was eating he heard a loud noise. The giant was coming home! Jack ran and hid in a basket. And just in time, for the giant was at the door!

As the giant came in, he sniffed and roared, "Fee, fi, fo, fum! I smell the blood of an Englishman!"

"That's just your dinner you smell," said the woman. "Sit down and eat."

So the giant ate his dinner. Then he got out a bag of gold and began to count it. After a while the giant fell asleep.

Jack had been watching the giant through a hole in the basket. Now Jack crawled out of the basket. He took the gold and climbed down the beanstalk.

Jack's mother was happy when she saw the gold. Now they had money for food and clothes.

Jack helped his mother in the garden for a week. Then he climbed the beanstalk again.

As before, Jack asked the woman for food. And, as before, she gave him something to eat. Jack ate the food quickly and hid in the basket.

Soon the giant came in and sniffed and roared, "Fee, fi, fo, fum! I smell the blood of an Englishman!"

"That's just your dinner you smell," said the woman. "Sit down and eat."

After the giant ate his dinner, he brought out a hen. He put the hen on the table and it laid a golden egg. After a while the giant fell asleep.

Jack crawled out of the basket, took the hen, and climbed down the beanstalk.

Jack's mother was happy when she saw the hen lay golden eggs. Now they had enough gold for the rest of their lives.

Jack worked in the garden for a week. Then he decided to climb the beanstalk again.

When he reached the top, the woman fed him again. Jack ate quickly and hid in the basket.

Jack had just finished when the giant came in the door. The giant sniffed and roared, "Fee, fi, fo, fum! I smell the blood of an Englishman!"

"That's just your dinner you smell," said the woman. "Sit down and eat."

After the giant had eaten his dinner, he got out a beautiful golden harp. He put it on the table. "Play," he said. The magic harp played a beautiful song. The giant fell asleep.

Jack crawled out of the basket. He took the harp and started for the beanstalk. But suddenly the harp shouted, "Master! Master!"

The giant woke and saw Jack. He ran after Jack. But just as he reached out to grab Jack, the giant tripped and fell. Jack climbed down the beanstalk as fast as he could, yelling, "Mother! Mother! Bring the ax!" Jack could hear the giant coming down the beanstalk after him.

When Jack reached the bottom, his mother gave
him an ax. Quickly Jack chopped down the
beanstalk. It crashed to the ground. And that was the
end of the giant.

Now Jack and his mother had everything they
would ever need. They had their house and their
garden. They had gold to buy food and clothes, a
hen to lay golden eggs, and a harp to play songs for
them. And so they lived happily ever after.

130

## Think about the selection

1. Is the story "Jack and the Beanstalk" realism or fantasy? What makes you think as you do?
2. Read these sentences. Tell which happened first in the story, which happened second, and which happened third.

—Jack chopped down the beanstalk.

—A man gave Jack some magic beans.

—Jack climbed the beanstalk and saw a giant.

## Checkpoint 10 ▬▬▬▬▬▬▬▬▬▬

Tell which of the underlined words in each sentence have the same vowel sound.

1. Did the beans thrown down on the ground grow?
2. Did Jack know he could sell the cow in town?
3. Jack's mother took the gold and bought good food.

# String Beans

by Johanna Hurwitz

It was Sunday, and Grandma and Grandpa had come
for a visit. Everyone sat around the dinner table
smiling. Daddy sliced the roast beef while Mommy
passed the mashed potatoes and gravy. There was
also a large bowl filled with string beans.

"I don't want any beans," said Teddy as he pushed
his plate away.

"Of course you do," said Daddy. "Everyone likes
string beans."

"No!" said Teddy. "Not me!"

132

"Well," said Grandpa, "I can remember a time when I had to eat too many beans. It was a long time ago, when I was a boy your age.

"I lived in the country then. Next door to my house there was a woman and her son. You may have heard about him. His name was Jack."

"Jack? I don't know anyone named Jack," said Teddy's sister, Nora.

"Well," said Grandpa, "I never liked him too much. But let me tell you what happened one day. Jack's mother told him to take their cow to town and sell it. Only instead of selling it, he traded it away for some beans."

"*That* Jack!" shouted Nora and Teddy. "Grandpa, did you really know *that* Jack who had the beanstalk?"

"I sure did," answered Grandpa. "I thought you might have heard about him. He got awfully famous for being so foolish. He brought those beans home. But his mother was so angry she just threw them out the window and sent Jack upstairs to bed. We invited her to stay for supper. We even sent a sandwich back for Jack. They don't tell about it in any of the stories.

"In the morning I saw a huge thing growing outside Jack's house," said Grandpa.

"The beanstalk!" cried Teddy and Nora.

"Yes, that's right," said Grandpa. "I knocked on Jack's door and asked if he wanted to walk to school with me. But that boy said he was going to stay home and climb to the top of the beanstalk."

"To the giant!" shouted Nora.

"Fee-fi-fo-fum!" called Daddy as he passed the meat.

"What happened next?" asked Teddy.

"Well," said Grandpa, "the teacher was angry with Jack. He never paid attention in class or did his work. And now he was playing hooky as well."

"Is that like playing hockey?" asked Nora.

"Hooky is when you stay home from school and you aren't sick," explained Mommy.

"Right," said Grandpa. "There we all were studying away, and that naughty boy Jack was playing hooky. I was sure he would get in trouble. But when I came home from school that afternoon, there was Jack holding a bag of gold. He told me that he had found it at the top of the beanstalk. Everyone thought he was wonderful!

"And the next day Jack stayed home from school again. He climbed the beanstalk a second time, and he brought back . . ."

"A hen that could lay golden eggs!" shouted Teddy.

"Right!" said Grandpa. "And the next day he stayed home from school again. He got a golden harp, only this time the giant started to follow him down the beanstalk! So when Jack reached the bottom, he called to his mother to bring him an ax."

"And she did, and he chopped down the beanstalk," said Nora.

"Wrong!" said Grandpa. "All those books are wrong! Jack's mother wasn't home. But luckily I had just returned from school. I ran and got my ax, and I chopped down the beanstalk for him."

"Oh, Grandpa. That's wonderful," breathed Teddy.

"Did you see the giant?" asked Nora.

"Of course," said Grandpa. "They may not write about me in the story, but I was there."

"Then what happened?" asked Nora.

"Well," said Grandpa, "we were left with a huge beanstalk. It had so many beans on it that we picked for three weeks without stopping. Even Jack stopped being lazy and helped pick. We had string beans for dinner every night for a month. And string-bean soup for lunch and even string-bean cereal for breakfast in the morning.

"That was a long, long time ago, but I still think of it whenever I have string beans for dinner," Grandpa said.

"Teddy, where are your beans?" asked Grandma.

Teddy looked at his plate. He looked under the table. Then he smiled. "I guess I ate them," he said.

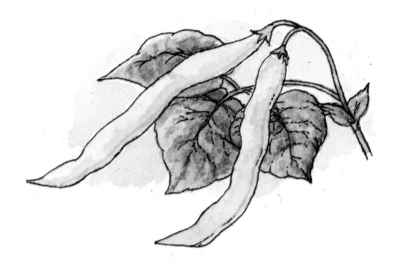

**Think about the selection**

1. What was the problem in the story "String Beans"?
2. Did Grandpa help solve the problem? How?
3. Why did Grandpa tell the story?
4. How was Grandpa's story different from the story on pages 123 to 130?
5. Why didn't Teddy realize that he was eating his string beans?

# John's Poor Memory

**John knew that he was supposed to get something at the store on the way home. His father had called him at Ben's house. But John and Ben had been watching TV ever since lunch. John didn't want to miss anything, so he didn't listen carefully to what his father said. Now John couldn't remember what he was supposed to buy.**

**What had his father said? John remembered something about getting white, not brown. And his dad had said, "Be sure to get the sliced kind." John laughed. Now he knew what he was supposed to bring home!**

### Think about skills

Sometimes you can use clues in a story to draw a conclusion or figure out something puzzling. For example, there were two clues to what John was to get. (1) He was to get white, not brown. (2) It was the sliced kind. These clues help you draw the conclusion that John was to get some bread.

In stories, one thing may cause something else to happen. This is called a cause-effect relationship. Why did John's father call him? Because he wanted John to bring home some bread.

1. Why did John forget what his dad told him?
2. Did the story happen on a school day? What clue helped you draw this conclusion?

*11: Teach*

## Practice skills

Juanita laughed out loud! Her little brother Alberto was on the kitchen table again. A chair was lying on its side nearby. As usual, Alberto couldn't get down. He was ready to cry.

"You've done it again!" Juanita said. "For a 15-month-old, you sure can climb!"

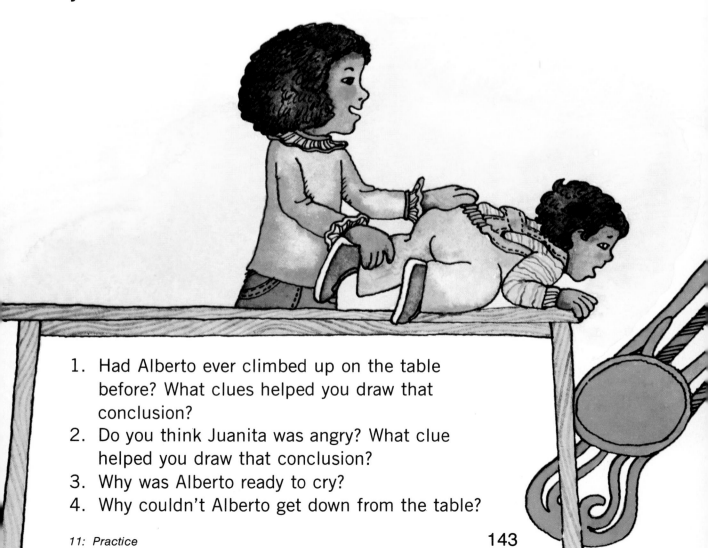

1. Had Alberto ever climbed up on the table before? What clues helped you draw that conclusion?
2. Do you think Juanita was angry? What clue helped you draw that conclusion?
3. Why was Alberto ready to cry?
4. Why couldn't Alberto get down from the table?

# Mariko Goes to Camp

11: Apply

by Judy Delton

*Have you ever been afraid to do something new? Sometimes we all are afraid to do something, but pretty soon we get used to it. And often we learn to like what we were once afraid of. This story tells about a girl named Mariko who goes to camp for the first time.*

One day my parents said, "Mariko, you might like to go away to camp this summer."

"Go away?" I said. "What is camp anyway?"

"Camp is sleeping in a tent and singing around a campfire at night. You hike through the woods and look at wild flowers. You find interesting rocks. You ride horses and swim."

"I won't know anyone," I said. "It won't be any fun."

"Try it and see," said my parents. "We think you'll like it."

145

On Monday I got on the bus for camp. I didn't know
any of the children. It was a long ride and I felt
lonely.

After a while we came to a place where there were
lots of trees. "Here we are!" said the driver. We all
got off the bus. We looked around for a good spot to
put up our tents. Miss Foster, our camp leader,
helped us set them up.

That evening after dinner we had a campfire. We roasted marshmallows. One of mine fell in the fire, but a girl named Julie gave me one of hers.

At night it was very dark inside the tent. I heard a loud flapping noise right near me. It sounded scary. "What is that?" I shouted, sitting up on my cot. I bumped my head on the tent pole.

"Bats," said Miss Foster. "They won't bother us."

In the morning we went fishing. Julie couldn't get her worm on the hook. I helped her. We caught a lot of fish. For lunch Miss Foster fried them. They tasted great.

In the afternoon we hiked in the woods. Julie and I took turns holding the branches back so they didn't scratch our faces. We found six different kinds of wild flowers. We didn't pick them. They looked prettier growing.

The next day we rode the horses. My horse was brown and had a white star and white feet. Its name was Beauty. After our ride, Julie and a girl named Carol and I fed bits of apple to our horses.

After lunch we went swimming. Julie and Carol and I had a race. We swam out to the rope and back. I won the first time. The next time Julie beat Carol and me. We had so much fun we didn't want to go in when Miss Foster called.

We had another campfire that night. It was fun singing songs together. The trees around us smelled good. And I could see some stars through the branches.

The next day it rained. We sang songs inside. Miss Foster played the guitar. She showed us how to play "Down in the Valley." We took turns. A girl named Jennifer told funny stories. She made us laugh a lot. We made peanut bars. We each ate six or seven.

*11: Apply*

At the end of the week Miss Foster said, "Get your things packed. Your parents will be here soon."

Julie and I fed the horses for the last time. I felt funny inside. I really didn't want camp to be over. Julie said she felt that way too.

Then my mom and dad drove up. I was glad to see them. I didn't know I had missed them so much. They hugged me. I guess they missed me too.

"Mom and Dad, this is my friend Julie," I said. "Can she come and visit us?"

"Hello, Julie," they said. "You're welcome to come visit anytime."

"And Mariko can visit me," said Julie.

"Come on, Mom and Dad," I said. "We want to show you the horses. And the place where we go swimming."

My mom and dad looked happy. "We thought you would like camp," they said.

"It was great," I said. "Can I come back next year?"

## Think about the selection

1. What sometimes happens when a person tries something new?
2. Who was Miss Foster?
3. What things did Miss Foster do that helped Mariko and the other girls like camp?
4. What scared Mariko after she went to bed on the first night at camp?

## Checkpoint 11

1. How can you tell that Mariko's parents wanted her to go to camp?
2. Why didn't Mariko want to go to camp?
3. What things in the story tell you that Mariko and Julie liked each other?
4. How did Mariko's parents know that Mariko liked camp?
5. Why did the campers stay inside the day after the second campfire?

# Facts at a Glance

A bar graph gives you information in a way that is easy to see and easy to read. Warren School has four baseball teams. The bar graph below shows the number of games won by each team. The title of the bar graph tells what information you can find in it. The numbers across the bottom of the graph tell the number of games won. And the names of the team captains are along the side.

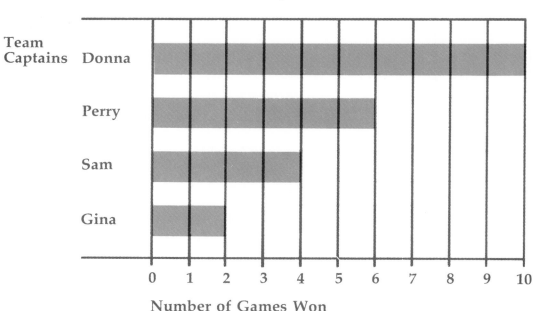

**Baseball Games Won by Warren School Teams**

Team Captains

Number of Games Won

Which bar is the longest? What name is next to the longest bar?

You can see that the bar next to Donna's name is the longest. That means that Donna's team won the most games.

1. Whose team won the fewest games? How can you tell?

Donna's team won ten games. So the bar by Donna's name is drawn out to the line above the number ten.

How many games did Perry's team win? If you said six, then you know how to read the bar graph!

Which two teams won more than five games? How many games did those teams win together? Use the graph to find out how many games each of those teams won. Then add the two numbers.

2. How many games did Sam's team win?
3. Which teams won more games than Sam's team?
4. Which teams won fewer games than Sam's team?
5. Which teams won more than three games?
6. Which teams won fewer than nine games?
7. How many games did all four teams win together?

## Practice skills

Mr. Ling's class made the bar graph below. It shows the ages of the children in his class. Use the bar graph to answer the questions.

1. What do the numbers at the bottom of the bar graph tell you? What do the numbers along the side tell you?
2. How old are most of the children?
3. Are more children 7 years old or 8 years old?
4. How many children are 10 years old?
5. How many children are younger than 10?

**Ages of Children in Mr. Ling's Class**

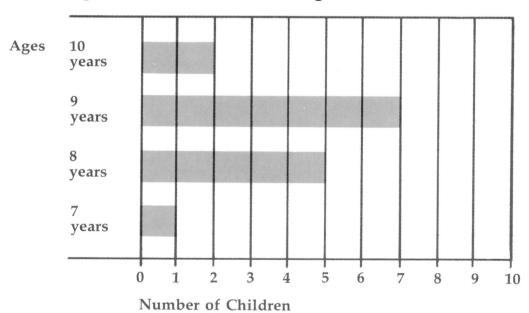

154

# POLLUTION!

by Polly Sanders

At school Debbie and her
friends were learning
about pollution. They
learned about things
that make the air dirty.
They learned about
things that make the
water dirty.

Debbie said, "I know another kind of pollution. It's all around us." The others wanted to know more about it. But Debbie wouldn't tell. She just said, "Look out the window."

The children looked out. Sure enough, there it was.

LITTER!

There were papers all over the schoolyard. It looked awful.

Debbie said, "Litter is a kind of pollution, I think." Then she said, "We don't have to throw things on the ground. And when we see litter, we can do something about it."

"Great idea!" said Carlos. "That's one kind of pollution we kids can help get rid of!"

The other children agreed. Mr. Tanaka, their teacher, said, "It's a fine idea. It can be a class project. Let's see who picks up the most papers. We'll keep a record of how many each of you picks up."

When recess time came, Debbie and her friends ran outside. They began to pick up the papers that littered the schoolyard. When they got through, they counted the papers they had picked up.

There was a big trash can at the corner of the building. The children dumped all the papers into the can. Then everyone turned around for one last look at the schoolyard.

"It looks great now!" said Tai.

"See, we *can* make a difference!" said Bob.

**Think about the selection**

1. Which sentence tells the main idea of the story?
2. Which sentence supports that main idea?

A. Children can pick up litter.
B. Children can do something about pollution.
C. Debbie talked about pollution.

158

# Checkpoint 12

1. Read the title of the bar graph below. What information will you find in the graph?
2. What do the numbers along the bottom of the graph tell you? What information is given along the left side of the graph?
3. Did Carlos or Debbie pick up more papers?
4. Who picked up the most papers? How can you tell?
5. Who picked up less than six papers?

**Papers Children Picked Up**

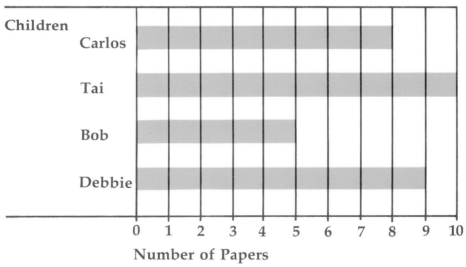

Number of Papers

# A Day at the Aquarium

One snowy day Kim went to the aquarium. The seals were swimming slowly in endless circles. Kim had taken two crusty loaves of bread for them. She was careful not to fall when she threw the bread into the water. After the bread had all been eaten, two playful seal calves begged for more.

The dolphins were beautiful. They were splashing and sliding off shelves at one end of their pool. They jumped for fish the trainer threw. The trainer pretended she had forgotten to feed the biggest dolphin. Then, with a careless move, she kicked a shiny fish into the water. The dolphin grabbed it and quickly ate it. Kim laughed happily. The dolphins were the funniest animals she had ever seen.

## Think about skills

Many words in the story have suffixes or endings. If you find a word that you don't know in a story, look to see if the word has a suffix or an ending. Finding the root word can help you understand what the longer word is.

» When you pronounce a word with a suffix, remember that a suffix usually adds a syllable to a root word. «

Two of the suffixes used in the story are *y* and *less*. The root word in *careless* is *care*.

1. What is the root word in *endless*?

   The root word in *crusty* is *crust*.

2. What is the root word in *snowy*?

   What are the root words in *seals, slowly, jumped, splashing,* and *playful*? If you said *seal, slow, jump, splash,* and *play,* you were right.

3. What are the root words in *dolphins, careful, laughed, eaten,* and *quickly*?

» Sometimes a change is made in a root word before a suffix or ending is added. The final consonant may be doubled. «

   What are the root words in *swimming, forgotten,* and *begged*? If you said *swim, forgot,* and *beg,* you were right.

4. What are the root words in *biggest* and *grabbed*?

≫ The final *e* of a root word may be dropped before a suffix or ending is added. ≪

The root word in *taken* is *take*.

5. What are the root words in *sliding* and *shiny*?

≫ The final *y* of a root word may be changed to *i* before a suffix or ending is added. ≪

The root word in *happily* is *happy*.

6. What is the root word in *beautiful*?

≫ If a root word ends in *f* or *fe*, the *f* or *fe* may be changed to *v* before a suffix or ending is added. ≪

The root words in *loaves* and *shelves* are *loaf* and *shelf*.

7. What is the root word in *calves?*

## Practice skills

What is the root word in each underlined word?

1. The largest dolphin jumped higher than the others.
2. The red scarves are prettier than the blue ones.
3. They hurried to cross the muddy field.
4. It's restful to lie under the leafy trees.
5. Did she finally sharpen the knives?
6. The boys were wearing sleeveless sweaters.

# Well!
# Why Didn't You Say So?

by Jo Anne Wold

Willie was gone! John looked under the picnic table. He looked inside the garage. He called and whistled. Finally John said, "I wonder where Willie went?"

But nobody knew. Not his mother and not his father. "You go look for Willie," his mother said.

So John went walking, walking, until he came to a man raking lemon leaves. "Have you seen Willie?" John asked.

"What does he look like?" asked the man.

"He's mostly brown," John answered.

"No, I haven't seen him," the man said, and he went on raking leaves.

From *Well! Why Didn't You Say So?* by Jo Anne Wold. Text © 1975 by Jo Anne Wold. Reprinted by permission of Albert Whitman & Company.

*13: Apply*

163

John kept on walking. Soon he saw three girls, all roller-skating in a driveway. "Have you seen Willie?" John called.

"What does he look like?" one girl asked.

"He's mostly brown with a long tail with white on it."

"Oh, no!" the girls answered together. "We haven't seen Willie."

John kept on walking. It wasn't long before he saw the ice-cream woman in her truck. "Hello," John called. "Have you seen Willie?"

164

"Chocolate, butter brickle, and peach," the ice-cream woman answered, leaning out of the truck window.

"No, no," John said. "I don't want ice cream. I want Willie. Have you seen him?"

"Oh, no," the woman said as she rang the bell on the ice-cream truck.

"Are you sure?" John asked. "You don't even know what he looks like."

"Well, what does he look like?" the woman asked.

"He's mostly brown. And he has a long tail with white on it. And he has one blue eye and one brown eye," John said.

"I haven't seen Willie," the woman said as she slowly drove away.

John kept on walking until he came to a small house among tall trees. A woman with a red scarf on her head was feeding the birds. "Hello," John called. "Have you seen Willie?"

"What does Willie look like?" the woman asked.

"He's mostly brown. And he has a long tail with white on it. One blue eye and one brown eye. And he is this tall," John said, measuring to his waist.

"Oh, my goodness, no," the woman said. "I haven't seen him." She shook her head sadly.

John's feet dragged. Where had Willie gone?

There was one more place to go. If Willie wasn't there, then he was gone forever. John hurried to the service station. A man at the service station was filling a car with gas. "Have you seen Willie?" John asked.

"What does Willie look like?" the man wanted to know.

John took a deep breath. "He's mostly brown. And he has a long tail with white on it. One blue eye and one brown eye. About this tall, with a red collar."

"Nope," the man said. "I haven't seen him. I haven't seen him at all."

So that was that. John turned toward home.

When John came to the small house among the tall trees, the woman who had been feeding the birds poked her head out of the window. "Did you find your pony?" she called.

"My pony! I'm not looking for a pony," John shouted. "I'm looking for my dog."

"Your dog? I declare! Why didn't you say so?" the woman exclaimed.

Pretty soon he saw the ice-cream truck. The ice-cream woman called, "Did you find your goat?"

"My goat! I'm not looking for a goat," John said. "I'm looking for my dog."

"Your dog!" the ice-cream woman said, and rang the bell. "Why in the world didn't you say so?"

*13: Apply*

John passed the girls with roller skates. They were sitting under a tree, sipping ice-cream sodas. "Did you find your squirrel?" they called together.

"My squirrel! I'm not looking for a squirrel. I'm looking for my D-O-G," and he spelled it out for them, just like that.

The girls laughed and asked, "Well, why didn't you say so?"

Finally John was back where he'd started. More leaves had fallen from the lemon tree. The man raking the leaves was still at work. "Did you find your cat?" he asked.

"My cat! I'm not looking for a cat. I'm looking for my dog. D-O-G," John said as loudly as he dared.

The man leaned on his rake and laughed. "A dog! A D-O-G. Well, why didn't you say so? Is he brown, with a long tail with white on it? With one blue eye and one brown eye? About this tall, and wearing a red collar?"

"Yes!" John shouted. "That's Willie."

"Oh? I found a dog like that, and I put him in my garage," the man said.

"Well, why didn't you say so?" John asked.

"You didn't ask," the man said.

## Think about the selection
1. What was the problem in this story?
2. How was the problem solved?
3. What did John do to try to find Willie?
4. How could John have solved the problem sooner?
5. How did John feel when he couldn't find Willie?
6. How do you think he felt when the man said that Willie was in the garage?

## Checkpoint 13
1. What are the root words in these words?

| | | |
|---|---|---|
| birds | leaves | shouted |
| dragged | mostly | sipping |
| feeding | poked | sitting |
| hurried | raking | walked |

2. John could have told everyone that Willie had floppy ears. What is the root word in *floppy?*
3. When John didn't find Willie at the gas station, he thought it was hopeless. What is the root word in *hopeless?*

# Spring Whispers

by Avis Witherbee

The winter was nearly over. The wind whispered
to the white rabbits who were beginning to turn
brown,
"It's coming!"

The rabbits knew what it meant and they started
to dance.

Moving quietly, the wind whispered to the
sleeping bears,
"It's coming!"

The bears woke up and yawned. They knew too.

175

In the snow-covered field the groundhogs peeked out. They looked around but did not see their shadows.

Blowing softly, the wind whispered in the ground-hog's ears,
"It's coming!"

And the groundhogs felt happy.

Warmly the wind blew across the earth and touched the tulips. The wind whispered,
"It's coming!"

The tulips peeked out from under the snow.

Gently the whistling wind whispered to the birds,
"It's coming!"

It was not long before a big fat robin appeared
and sang.

The wind touched the lilacs and whispered,
"It's coming!"

They knew too and started to grow.

From a hole in the old stone wall the garden snakes
heard the wind whisper,
"It's coming!"

Slowly they uncurled.

Then the wind whispered to the sun,
"It's coming!"

176

The sun knew and winked. It shone down so brightly that the snow melted.

The warm air hugged the earth and everything turned green.

Everyone was happy.

Spring was here!

## Think about the selection

1. Which sentence below tells the main idea of "Spring Whispers"?
   Everything turned green.
   The animals felt happy.
   Spring is coming.

2. What are the root words in these words?
   beginning   softly   coming   hugged   whistling

# Rachel's Puzzle

**Rachel put her jelly sandwich in her pocket and went out the open kitchen door. When she got to the barn, she saw that one stirrup on her saddle was broken. That was a puzzle! Rachel didn't know how it had happened. But it made her sad because she wanted to ride out to the desert.**

## Think about skills

The numbered sentences below will help you divide longer words into syllables.

**»**1. If two or more consonant letters are between two vowel letters, the word is usually divided between the consonants to form syllables. But a word is not usually divided between such blends as *pl, sp,* or *tw,* nor between *ck, ch, sh,* or *th.*

2. If one consonant letter is between two vowel letters, the consonant may go with the first vowel letter or it may go with the second vowel letter to form a syllable.

3. If a word ends in *le* and has one or more consonant letters before the *le,* at least one consonant usually goes with the *le* to form a syllable.**«**

*14: Teach*

The words below are from the story on page 179.
Each word has two syllables. One syllable in each
word is accented. This is an accent mark '. An accent
mark is after the syllable that is accented in each
word. The numbers match the numbered sentences on
page 179.
1. jel'ly
2. o'pen      des'ert
3. puz'zle

Decide which numbered sentence on page 179 each
word below matches.

bro'ken      sad'dle      pock'et
stir'rup      teach'er      fin'ish

The numbered sentences will help you with vowel
sounds in words and accented syllables.

>> 1.  If one vowel letter in a word or accented syllable
       is followed by one or more consonant letters, the
       vowel letter usually stands for a short vowel sound.
       This is not so if the consonant after the vowel is _r._
       Then the vowel sound may be different.
2.  If there are two vowel letters together in a word or
    accented syllable, they usually stand for a long
    vowel sound.
3.  If the only vowel letter in a word or accented
    syllable is at the end, the vowel letter usually
    stands for a long vowel sound. <<

## Practice skills

Jack put the bacon on the stove so it would cook slowly.
Then he made a peanut butter sandwich and put tea in a
thermos bottle. The cat rubbed against Jack's legs so
he would notice that there was no food in its dish. So
Jack got food for the cat. After he ate his bacon, Jack
went out to check the cattle.

check     butter     thermos     tea     peanut

1. Which words have two syllables?

bot'tle     pea'nut     so           cat'tle     why
ba'con      paint       nee'dle      top         toe

2. Which words match number 1 at the bottom of
   page 180?
3. Which words match number 2 on page 180?
4. Which words match number 3 on page 180?

# Which One Is Mine?

by Barbara Walker

*The characters in the play are the cat, the rabbit, and the fox. The cat and the rabbit are good friends. One day they find a big piece of cheese in the forest. The cat and the rabbit both like cheese very much.*

CAT: You break the cheese into two pieces. Then we will each have some.

RABBIT: I will make both pieces of cheese exactly the same size. (*The rabbit breaks the cheese into two pieces. But one piece of cheese is a little bigger than the other. The cat grabs the larger piece of cheese.*)

CAT: This one is mine!

RABBIT: No, it isn't. It's mine!

Adapted from *Humpty Dumpty's Magazine.* Copyright © 1962 by Humpty Dumpty, Inc. Reprinted by permission.

*14: Apply*

*(A fox walks by. The rabbit talks to the fox.)*

**RABBIT:** The cat and I have two pieces of cheese. I
want the bigger piece of cheese, but the cat
wants the bigger one too. Which one is
mine?

**FOX:** That's easy, I'll bite the bigger piece of cheese so they will both be the same size. *(The fox bites the cheese, but takes too much.)*

**CAT:** Now the *other* one is bigger!

**FOX:** That's all right. I will bite that one so they will both be the same size. (*The fox eats some of the other piece of cheese. But the fox bites off too much again.*)

**RABBIT:** Now the *first* one is bigger again.

**FOX:** I will bite it again. Then they will be the same size. (*This time the fox eats the whole piece of cheese.*)

**CAT:** But it's all gone now!

**FOX:** So it is. Now I will have to eat the other piece of cheese. Then they will surely be the same size. (*The fox eats the other piece of cheese and then runs away.*)

**RABBIT:** Now both pieces of cheese are gone!

**CAT:** Yes, and which one was mine?

**RABBIT:** It doesn't matter now. They are both gone, and we don't have any cheese at all.

**CAT:** From now on, let's solve our problems ourselves!

# Think about the selection

1. Is "Which One Is Mine?" realism or fantasy? Explain your answer.
2. What problem did the cat and the rabbit have?
3. How was their problem solved?
4. Do you think that was a good way to solve the problem? Explain your answer.

## Checkpoint 14

1. Which of the words below have two syllables?
   a. into    c. fox    e. little
   b. matter    d. size    f. solve
2. Which numbered sentence on page 179 does each of these words match?
   a. a way'    c. lit'tle    e. eas'y
   b. mat'ter    d. prob'lems    f. rab'bit
3. Which numbered sentence on page 180 does each of these words match?
   a. we    c. larg'er    e. prob'lems
   b. big'ger    d. cheese    f. eas'y

# Paper Animals

You can make paper animals like the ones the
children have in the photographs on pages 183
to 187. You can use the animals to put on the
play "Which One Is Mine?"

## Cat

**You need:**
colored paper
heavy twine
a button
crayons
ruler
scissors

1. Draw a cat's face and
   stripes on a piece of
   colored paper as
   shown in the picture.
   Cut out the ears on
   the dotted lines. Make
   small holes at each
   end of the paper where
   the small circles are.

Adapted from *Card and Cardboard* © 1969 Santillana,
S. A. de Ediciones. English translation 1970,
Macdonald & Co. (Publishers) Ltd. Reprinted by
permission of Ediciones Altea, Macdonald & Co.
(publishers) Ltd. and Franklin Watts, Inc.

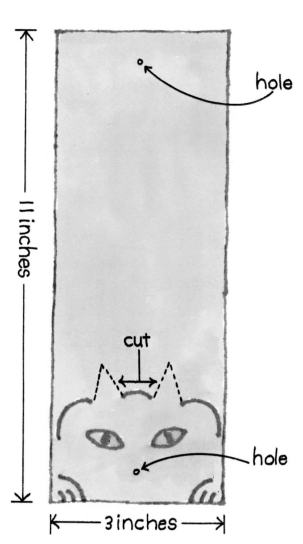

2. Thread the twine through the button as shown. Cut some short pieces of twine. Knot them right behind the button.

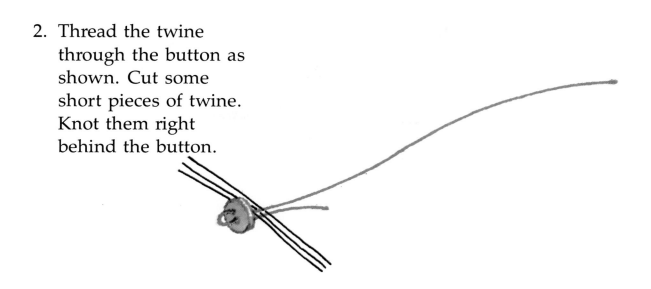

3. Thread the twine through the cat's body as it shows in the picture. Pull the twine tight so the cat's body curves. Tie a knot in the twine to hold the shape of the curve.

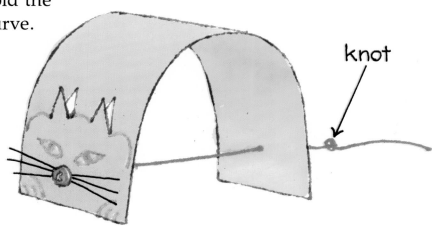

knot

## Rabbit

**You need:**
an empty cardboard tube
colored paper
crayons
paste
scissors

1. Draw shapes on the
   colored paper like
   those shown here.
   The circle is the
   rabbit's head. Draw
   eyes and a nose on it.
   The four big shapes
   are the rabbit's ears
   and feet. The two
   small shapes are the
   rabbit's arms. Cut out
   the shapes.

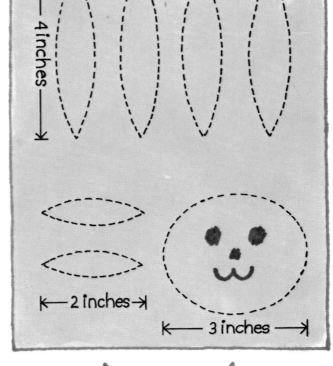

2. Paste the ears onto the
   back of the head.

190

3. Cut a slit on each side of one end of the tube. Slip the head into the slits.

cut

4. Put the feet and arms onto the tube. Bend the arms in half and paste the upper half only. Paste the top ends of the feet inside the tube and bend the bottom ends forward.

fold on dotted line

paste

191

# Fox

**You need:**
colored paper
crayons
ruler
scissors

1. Measure and draw this shape on a piece of colored paper. Draw eyes and a nose as shown in the picture. Cut on the dotted lines.

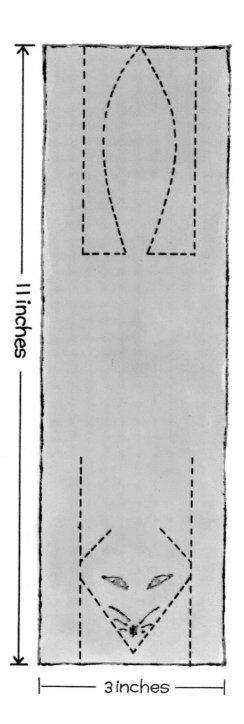

11 inches

3 inches

2. Fold on the dotted
   lines in this picture.
   Fold the legs down.
   Then fold the feet
   forward. Fold the neck
   up. Then fold the head
   down.

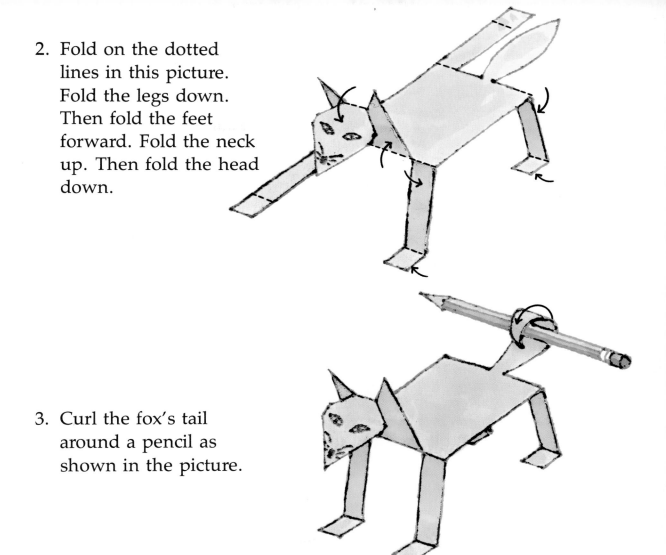

3. Curl the fox's tail
   around a pencil as
   shown in the picture.

**Think about the selection**
1. Which of the three paper animals can be made
   from these parts?
   colored paper, twine, button
2. Put these steps for making the rabbit in order.
   a. Paste the feet onto the cardboard tube.
   b. Cut out the head, ears, and feet.
   c. Bend the feet so the rabbit will stand up.

# Using Your Glossary

The Glossary in the back of this book can help you find out what words mean and how to pronounce them.

You might find this sentence as you read: *All the characters breathed, "Oh, no!"* You might not know what *characters* means. But you know that the entry words in a glossary are root words. So you could take off the ending *s* and find the meaning of *character* in your Glossary.

What could you do if you didn't know how to pronounce *breathed?* You could use the Glossary to find out! Find the root word *breathe* in the Glossary and look at the pronunciation. Is the vowel sound in *breathe* like the vowel sound in *let* or the first vowel sound in *equal?*

Now read the rest of the entry for *breathe.* Which definition tells what *breathed* means in the sentence *All the characters breathed, "Oh, no!"* Read the sentence after definition 3. It helps you understand the third meaning of *breathe.*

1. What are the guide words on the page on which you found the entry word *breathe?*
2. Which definition of *breathe* tells what the word means in the following sentence?
   He was breathing hard after his fast run.

3. Find the entry for *character* in the Glossary. Besides the definitions, what else in the entry helps you understand the different meanings of *character?*
4. Find the pronunciation of the entry word *aisle* in the Glossary. Is the vowel sound in *aisle* like the vowel sound in *age* or the vowel sound in *ice?*
5. What entry word would you look up to find the meaning of *describing?*

## Practice skills

Use the Glossary in the back of your book to answer these questions.

1. Find the pronunciation of the entry word *desert.* Is the first vowel sound in *desert* like the one in *let* or like the first vowel sound in *equal?*
2. What are the guide words on the page on which you found *desert?*
3. Which definition of *litter* tells what the word means in the following sentence?
   The black puppy was the smallest in the litter.
4. Besides the definition, what else in the entry for *litter* helped you understand the meaning in the sentence in number 3?
5. What entry word would you look up to find the definition of *sharply?*
6. Find the pronunciation of the entry word *shield.* Is the vowel sound in *shield* like the vowel sound in *ice* or the first vowel sound in *equal?*

# She Did What She Wanted

Today Christine Haycock is a doctor in New Jersey. But when she was a child, she wanted to be a baseball player.

"I was the only girl in my neighborhood," Dr. Haycock says. "I used to play baseball with the boys. I followed my big brother all over the place. He did not like it much. And he *really* did not like it when we played baseball. When we would choose up sides, I was picked before he was!"

When she was 13, Christine tried to get on her high-school baseball team. But the school would not let a girl play. Then a New Jersey semipro team heard about her. The team signed her on.

"They let me on the team so they would get their name in the papers," Dr. Haycock says. "But I did not mind. I would go out and catch flies before the game. Then, if my team got very far behind, they would let me play."

Some people thought she should stop playing ball. These people did not think girls should play baseball. "My brother said I was a disgrace to the family!" says Dr. Haycock.

Adapted and reprinted by permission from *Scholastic Sprint,* © 1976 by Scholastic Magazines, Inc. and Dr. Christine Haycock.

*15: Apply*

But Christine liked baseball. And she kept on playing.

Christine also played on a girls' softball team. She would either catch or pitch for that team. She used a very fast pitch. It was called a riser. At one game, one of her pitches was clocked at 65 miles an hour!

"I grew to love softball," Dr. Haycock says. "But it was never quite the same as baseball. I always felt I should have had the chance to play big-time ball."

Now Christine is a doctor. And she still uses a lot of what she learned playing ball.

"I enjoy being a doctor," she says. "And I still do many of the things I did as a ball player. I need to know how to make up my mind—fast. And I have to have good control of my hands.

"To be good at anything," Dr. Haycock says, "you have to train for it. This is true for doctors. And it is true for baseball players."

## Think about the selection

1. Is "She Did What She Wanted" fact or fiction? Why do you think so?
2. Christine's brother said Christine was a disgrace to the family because she played baseball. Do you think he was being fair to his sister? Why do you think as you do?
3. Why do you think Christine didn't get a chance to play big-time baseball? Do you think this was fair? Tell why you think as you do.
4. Do you think Dr. Christine Haycock is the kind of person who would keep on trying to do what she wanted in spite of what other people said or did to stop her? Explain your answer.

## Checkpoint 15

Use the Glossary to answer these questions.

1. Find the pronunciation of the entry word *convenient.* Is the first vowel sound in *convenient* like the vowel sound in *hot* or like the first vowel sound in *about?*
2. Besides the definitions in the entry for *convenient,* what else helps you understand the different meanings of the word?
3. What are the guide words on the page on which you found the entry word *convenient?*
4. Which definition of *appear* tells what the word means in the following sentence?
   The dog appeared to be lost so Paul took it to the animal shelter.
5. What entry word would you look up to find the word *controlled* in the Glossary?

# 16

Root words
Endings
Prefixes

# Matt's Test

Matt was going to have a test on prefixes. But he felt very unsure of himself. What did he, Matt Greene, know about prefixes? Matt did not have much time left to study. So he was rereading the pages in his book on prefixes. "Maybe that will help," Matt thought.

>> A prefix is added at the beginning of a word to make another word with a different meaning. <<

The prefix *re* usually means "again."
So the word *reglue* means "glue again."

The prefix *un* means "not" or "do the opposite of." So the word *uneven* means "not even." And the word *unlock* means "do the opposite of lock."

"That's not so hard," Matt said to himself. "These rules make it easy to understand how adding a prefix makes another word with a different meaning. Maybe the test won't be so bad."

# Think about skills

Part of the test Matt took is on this page. Read it and see if you agree with Matt's answers.

1. Sam helped Tony <u>unbutton</u> his coat.
   The root word in *unbutton* is <u>button</u>.
   *Unbutton* means
   ☐ button again
   ☒ do the opposite of button

2. Marla spilled some juice on her paper so she had to <u>redo</u> it.
   The root word in *redo* is <u>do</u>.
   *Redo* means
   ☒ do again    ☐ not do

3. Sonia <u>refilled</u> the bird feeder last week.
   The root word in *refilled* is <u>fill</u>.
   *Refilled* means
   ☐ not filled    ☒ filled again

All of Matt's answers are right. He knew the meanings of the prefixes *un* and *re*. So he could figure out the meanings of the underlined words.

Matt also knew how to find the root words in the underlined words. First he took off the prefix *un* or *re*. But he also knew that some words have a suffix or ending added to them. So Matt took off the prefix *re* and the ending *ed* to find the root word in *refilled*.

Now see if you can answer these questions from Matt's test.

1. Is a prefix added at the beginning or the end of a word?
2. What do the prefixes *un* and *re* mean?
3. What are the root words in *unsure* and *retied*?
4. What do the words *unsure* and *retied* mean?

## Practice skills

Trudy <u>unrolled</u> the paper so she could read it.
1. What is the root word in *unrolled*?
2. What does *unrolled* mean?

Chris is <u>rewriting</u> his paper.
3. What is the root word in *rewriting*?
4. What does *rewriting* mean?

Fred thought it <u>unfair</u> that he couldn't have a dog.
5. What is the root word in *unfair*?
6. What does *unfair* mean?

When Kim cut the cake it was <u>uneven</u>.
7. What is the root word in *uneven*?
8. What does *uneven* mean?

*16: Teach/Practice*

# Tall Tina

by Muriel Stanek

When Tina was little, everybody at home called her Tiny Tina. But as she grew taller and taller and went to school, it was only Grandma who still called her Tiny Tina.

"Tiny, please find my glasses," Grandma would say.

"Here they are, Grandma," Tina would call. "Right up here on the shelf."

That would make Grandma smile, and she'd say, "My Tiny Tina is getting tall, and that's fine. There are lots of tall people in our family."

It was true. Most of Tina's family were tall. And Tina liked that. She was proud to look like her family.

From *Tall Tina* by Muriel Stanek. Text © 1970 by Muriel Stanek. Reprinted by permission of Albert Whitman & Company.

At school Tina was the tallest girl in her room. Most of the time this was fine with Tina. Her teacher would say, "Tina, please rearrange the paper on the top shelf in the cupboard."

"Not everyone can do that," Tina would tell herself.

Tina had long legs. She could run fast. On the way to school she would call to Robbie, "Bet you can't catch me!"

"You always win," Robbie would say. "That's because you have those long legs."

But sometimes, of course, Tina was unhappy about being tall. At school she was tired of sitting in the last seat in her row. At home she was getting too tall to squeeze down into her favorite hiding place under the little round table.

And because Tina was so tall, everyone expected her to act as grown-up as Beth. Beth was Tina's older sister. But Tina wasn't as grown-up as Beth.

204

One day a new boy named Jonathan moved into Tina's neighborhood. He was in her class at school. On the way home from school, Jonathan shouted, "Tina is a string bean—String Bean Tina!"

Some of the children laughed. Then somebody called, "Tall Tina! Look at Tall Tina!"

Tina ran home without looking back at anyone.

The next morning there was a note on Tina's desk. When she unfolded it, she read, "Tina is a—" and there was a picture of a giraffe.

Tears filled Tina's eyes. "It's not my fault if I'm tall," she said to herself. Then she slid down in her seat so she would look shorter.

That night Tina tried walking with her knees bent and her shoulders stooped.

"How come you're walking like that?" her sister Beth asked.

"I have to look shorter," Tina answered.

"Who cares if you're tall? Mother and Aunt Mary are tall. They don't care," Beth said.

But Tina did care. She couldn't help it.

Now nothing seemed as much fun to Tina as it had. She began to think everyone was laughing at her because she was tall. At recess she stayed inside.

206

One afternoon when Tina was walking home, she saw Jonathan behind her. She ran as fast as she could toward a big fence. She hid behind it and peeked out from between the boards.

As Jonathan came closer, she saw he was not running after her at all. Two boys were chasing him!

All at once Jonathan tripped, fell, and bumped his nose so hard it bled. There was a big red bump on his forehead.

While Tina watched, the two boys ran up and laughed at Jonathan. He had his hand to his nose and tears ran down his cheeks.

"Crybaby!" the boys yelled as they ran off.

Tina stayed behind the fence until
the two boys had gone. She was
all set to say, "Ha, ha, ha,
Jonathan. Serves you right! Now
you know how it feels to have
someone make fun of you."

But as Tina came over to Jonathan
she didn't yell at him after all. She
was surprised—she felt sorry for
Jonathan!

She handed him her handkerchief,
and he wiped his nose and slowly
got up. Tina helped him repack
his books in his book bag.

Tina and Jonathan walked down
the street together without saying
a word.

208

At Jonathan's house, they stood for a moment. Jonathan's nose had stopped bleeding, and the bump on his head didn't look too bad.

"Want to see my new kitten, Tina?" he asked.

Tina wondered if she had really heard Jonathan. For the first time he had used her right name and wasn't making fun of her.

"Maybe he isn't so bad after all," she thought. Still, she wasn't sure she really wanted to be friendly.

"My mother is waiting for me," she answered. "I'll stop and see your kitten some other time."

As she walked on toward home nobody called "Tall Tina!" or "String Bean!" That felt good.

The next morning Tina looked at her desk to see if there were any mean notes from Jonathan. There weren't any.

When she went outside she listened to hear if someone called teasing names. No one did.

A warm spring day came, and the class was on the playground.

The gym teacher said, "We're going to have relay races. Jonathan will be the captain of one team. Dora will be the captain of the other team. Captains, choose your teams!"

Dora chose Mark for her team. Then it was Jonathan's turn to choose.

"I choose you!" he said, pointing to Tina.

"Why should I be on his team?" Tina asked herself, but she walked slowly toward Jonathan.

The teams lined up. The shortest runners were first and the tallest last. Mark was last on Dora's team. Tina was last on Jonathan's team.

"Ready, set, GO!" called the gym teacher.

Dora and Jonathan raced to the fence and then back to the next runners in line. The teams were so evenly matched it was hard to tell which would win.

Waiting to run, Tina and Mark jumped up and down. Tina felt *she* had to win. Mark felt *he* had to win.

It was a close race right to the very end.

"Run, Tina, run!" yelled Jonathan. Tina ran as hard as she could— she had to beat Mark.

Tina's long legs carried her over the finish line just ahead of Mark. She had done it! She had won for her team!

Everybody cheered. Jonathan shouted "We won!" the loudest of all and gave Tina a big smile.

That night when Tina looked in the mirror at home, she stood straight and tall. She didn't stoop or slump. Being tall was a pretty good thing. She felt like herself again, glad to be in a tall family.

## Think about the selection

1. In the beginning of the story, how did Tina feel about being tall?
2. How did Tina feel about being tall after Jonathan moved into her neighborhood?
3. Do you think the note Jonathan wrote Tina was funny? Do you think Jonathan should have written it? Why do you think as you do?
4. How did Jonathan feel when he was teased?
5. What made Jonathan change his mind about Tina?
6. Why do you think Tina didn't go to see Jonathan's kitten?
7. At the end of the story, how did Tina feel about being tall?

## Checkpoint 16

unhappy        rearrange
unfolded      repack

1. What are the root words in the words above?
2. What does each word mean?

# GROWING: For Louis

It's tough being short.

Of course your father tells you not to worry,
But everyone else is giant, and you're just the
way you were.
And this stupid guy says, "Hey, shorty, where'd
you get the long pants?"
Or some smart beanpole asks how it feels to be
so close to the ants?
And the school nurse says to tell her again how
tall you are, when you've already told her.
Oh, my mother says there's really no hurry
And I'll grow soon enough.

But it's tough being short.

(I wonder if Napoleon got the same old stuff?)

Myra Cohn Livingston

214

# My Dog, Sam

"I just don't like the food you give me," Sam, my dog, says. "Why can't I eat the same food you do?" Sam says all the time. In fact, Sam complains so much that I wish I had never taught him to talk.

# Jim Comes Home

Terry watched the planes take off and land. She liked being at the airport. She was especially happy today. Her brother Jim was coming home.

*17: Teach*

—

215

## Think about skills

The paragraphs you just read are the beginnings of two stories. Both paragraphs are fiction. Both paragraphs are from made-up stories. But one story is fantasy and the other is realism.

The story about Sam, the dog, is fantasy. It is fantasy because it could never happen. The story about Terry, the girl at the airport, is realism. The story didn't happen, but it could happen.

Look at "Jack and the Beanstalk," pages 123–130, and "Tall Tina," pages 203–212. Both stories are fiction. Use the stories to answer the questions.

1. Which story is fantasy? How do you know?
2. Which story is realism? How do you know?
3. What is fantasy? What is realism?

## Practice skills

Use the stories "Well! Why Didn't You Say So?" pages 163–171, and "Which One Is Mine?" pages 182–186, to answer the questions.

1. Which story is realism? How do you know?
2. Which story is fantasy? How do you know?

# Melvin Gets His Wish

by Jean Pigeon

Melvin sat down on a park bench. He held his cat on his lap. The cat was shaking all over. "Don't be afraid, Waldo," Melvin said. "I chased that dog away. It won't bark at you any more."

Suddenly a woman appeared on the bench beside Melvin. "What's the matter with your cat?" she asked.

Melvin jumped. "Who are you?" he asked. "And where did you come from?"

217

"Who I am is easy," the woman said. "My name is Mrs. Rivera. Where I come from is harder." She looked sharply at Melvin. "I don't suppose you believe in fairy godmothers," she said.

"Of course not," Melvin answered. "Fairy godmothers are only in stories."

"Truth is stranger than fiction," said Mrs. Rivera.

"Besides, fairy godmothers in stories are always young and beautiful," said Melvin.

"Handsome is as handsome does," said Mrs. Rivera. "I asked what's the matter with your cat."

"A dog was chasing him," Melvin answered. "I chased the dog away. But Waldo is still scared. I wish Waldo were ten feet long! Then the dogs would be scared of *him!*"

"If that's what you want . . ." said Mrs. Rivera. She clapped her hands.

Waldo leaped out of Melvin's lap. And he started to grow. In a few seconds, the cat was ten feet long!

"WOW!" shouted Melvin. "Is that really Waldo?"

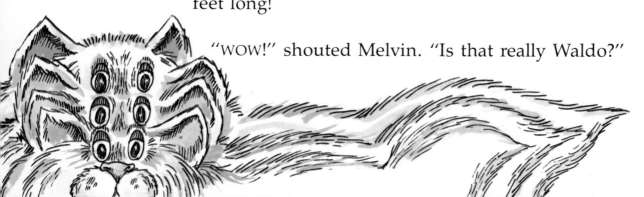

"Seeing is believing," said Mrs. Rivera. "Have a nice day." And she disappeared.

Melvin looked around for the woman. Then he heard a roar in his ears. It sounded like a jet plane. And something knocked him down. It was Waldo! He had tried to rub his head against Melvin's cheek. And he was purring.

Melvin got up. "Take it easy, Waldo," he said. "Come on. Let's go home."

When Melvin got home, his parents were making dinner. Melvin led Waldo into the kitchen.

"What's that?" Melvin's father yelled. He dropped a bowl of rice on the floor.

"What's that?" Melvin's mother yelled. She spilled a pan of gravy.

"It's just Waldo," Melvin said. "He's hungry."

Melvin's mother reached out and scratched Waldo's ear. Waldo swished his tail. He knocked all the dishes off the table. "Oh, no!" said Melvin's father.

Melvin got a big box of Cat Crunchies out of the cupboard. Waldo ate the whole box in two bites. Then he looked at the roast on the counter. He ate that in two bites too. "Oh, no!" said Melvin's mother.

"Get that cat out of here," both of Melvin's parents yelled.

That night Waldo jumped up on Melvin's bed. He curled up and went to sleep. There was no room for Melvin! Melvin tried to push Waldo off the bed. But he couldn't move the cat. Melvin had to sleep on the floor.

220

The next morning Waldo ate two boxes of
cereal, six cans of tuna fish, and Melvin's father's
soft-boiled egg. He drank three quarts of milk and
Melvin's mother's orange-flower tea. "Get that cat
out of here!" both of Melvin's parents yelled.

Melvin took Waldo to the park. He sat down on
a bench to think. Suddenly Mrs. Rivera was on the
bench beside him. "What's the matter now?" she
asked.

"I wish Waldo was cat-sized again," Melvin said.

"I wish you'd make up your mind," said Mrs. Rivera. She clapped her hands. And Waldo began to shrink. In a few seconds he was his old size.

Melvin hugged Waldo. "Thank you, Mrs. Rivera," he said. "This is the right size for Waldo to be."

"Sometimes it's best to leave well enough alone," said Mrs. Rivera. And she disappeared.

## Think about the selection

These words are from "Melvin Gets His Wish."

| | | |
|---|---|---|
| answered | clapped | chasing |
| shaking | hugged | leaped |
| stories | beautiful | making |
| tried | sharply | dropped |

1. Which words have no change in the spelling of the root word before an ending or suffix?
2. In which words was the final consonant in the root word doubled before an ending or suffix?
3. In which words was the final *e* in the root word dropped before an ending or suffix?
4. In which words was the final *y* in the root word changed to *i* before an ending or suffix?
5. What two words does each of these contractions or compounds stand for?

   softboiled     don't     cat-sized
6. Why did Melvin want Waldo to be ten feet long?
7. Why did Melvin want Waldo to be cat-sized again?

## Checkpoint 17

1. Is the story "Melvin Gets His Wish" realism or fantasy? How do you know?
2. What are some of the things that happened in the story that are realistic?

# Don't Be Late!

"Come straight home after school," Mr. Kent had told Jan.
"We have to leave for the baseball game at four o'clock.
If you don't come straight home, we'll be late for the
game."

But Jan forgot. On the way home from school, she
stopped at Keith's house to see his new puppy. Then she
remembered what her father had told her.

What could Jan do? She could walk home and be late or
she could call home to tell her parents where she was.

Jan decided to call her parents. They picked her up at
Keith's house and then they all went to the game. They
got there just in time.

224

## Think about skills

The problem in "Don't Be Late!" was that Jan forgot she was supposed to go home right after school. She should not have stopped at Keith's house. Her family would be late for the ball game if Jan didn't get home in time.

Jan thought of two things she could do to solve her problem. She could begin walking home and make everyone late. Or she could call and ask her parents to pick her up. Jan called her parents. This was a good solution to the problem because her family could still get to the ball game on time.

Think about the story "Lost and Found" on pages 86–92. Then answer the following questions.

1. What was the story problem? How was it solved?
2. Do you think Mrs. Lopez's solution was a good one? Why or why not? What else could she have done to solve the problem?
3. The house was very quiet after everyone went home with their lost things. How did Mrs. Lopez feel then?
4. Mrs. Lopez's neighbors came to see her after all the lost things had been returned. Do you think that was a nice thing to do? Why do you think as you do?

## Practice skills

"Julie, let me go with you," begged five-year-old Mike. "I won't get in the way. I can play baseball too. Please let me go."

"No, Mike, you're too little to play baseball," Julie said. She started toward the playground. When she looked back, she saw Mike sitting on the steps. He looked sad. Julie felt terrible.

Suddenly Julie remembered that many of the other baseball players had young brothers and sisters who often came along. They could play on the slide nearby. Mike could too.

Julie came running back to Mike. "Hey, Mike!" she called. "Go ask Mom if you can go with me."

1. What was the story problem? How was it solved?
2. Do you think this was the best way to solve the problem? Why or why not?
3. How did Julie feel when she looked back?
4. Why do you think Julie felt that way?

226

# The World's Greatest PET Show

by Nancy Garber

"But, Mother, what could go wrong at a pet show?" Janie asked.

"Just about anything," her mother said. "So please don't plan to have it here at the house. The Manleys won't like it, you know." Mr. and Mrs. Manley had just moved into the upstairs rooms of Janie's house.

"We could have the pet show out in the yard," Janie said. "That wouldn't bother Mr. and Mrs. Manley."

Adaptation of "The World's Greatest Pet Show" by Nancy Garber from *Wee Wisdom*, April 1976. © 1976 by Unity School of Christianity. Reprinted by permission.

*18: Apply*

Her mother thought that would be all right. So Janie told her friends. Jill would bring her rabbits and Jon his cat. Amy had a big dog, George, with a lot of hair over his eyes. Len would bring his white mice. Stephen had an ant farm, and Sarah's big black talking bird would be the hit of the show. The bird talked in long sentences. "See what a good-looking bird I am!" it often said.

Janie had only one worry. She didn't want Mr. and Mrs. Manley to be angry about the pet show. They didn't like noise. Then she had an idea. What if she asked them to be a part of the pet show? Maybe they would like it better. They could be the judges. She ran upstairs and knocked on their door.

On Saturday morning Janie's friends came with their pets. And right behind them came Mr. and Mrs. Manley. Janie had made colored ribbons into circles with the ends hanging down. These were the prizes that the Manleys would give out.

All the children stood proudly behind the pets. Mr. and Mrs. Manley walked up and down, looking carefully at each pet.

But suddenly the sky got darker. It began to rain. The Manleys and the children ran for the porch. It was a small porch, so no one had much room. With all the pets, it was really a tight squeeze. But Mr. and Mrs. Manley began to hand out the prizes.

"A red ribbon for the most hard-working animals,
Stephen's ants in the ant farm," said Mrs. Manley.

"A prize for the pet that talks in the longest sentences,
Sarah's black bird," said Mr. Manley.

Mrs. Manley walked over to hand the ribbon to Sarah.
Sarah reached out for it and knocked over the bird's
cage. "See what a good-looking bird I am!" the big
black bird called. It flew up to the ceiling. Then it
came down and landed on top of Jon's cat. The cat
got excited and leaped into the air. That knocked over
the white mice's cage. The mice ran out and under
and into everything to find a place to hide.

230

George, the dog, ran in circles and barked. Jill's
rabbits sat quietly in their box until the cat leaped in
among them. Then they left in a hurry.

All at once Mr. Manley began shaking his leg and
making a squeaking sound. No—the squeaking sound
was coming from a white mouse that had run up his
pants' leg.

"Oh, no!" thought Janie. "This pet show is coming
apart! What will the Manleys think of all this noise?
They might be sorry they ever moved here."

Finally, Sarah caught her black bird and put it in its
cage. The dog flopped down on the floor for a rest.
Len caught his mice, and Jill got her rabbits into
their box. The cat, seeing that the fun was over, went
back to Jon. Mr. and Mrs. Manley began to give out
more prizes.

"For the most clever cage escape, Sarah's black bird," said Mrs. Manley. "And for the greatest flying leap into a box of rabbits, Jon's cat."

"For the fastest pants'-leg climbing, Len's white mice," said Mr. Manley. "And for the most happy barking, George, Amy's dog."

Mrs. Manley gave the last prize to Jill's rabbits. "For the quickest jumps from a box," she said.

Janie could hardly believe her ears. Mr. Manley was being so funny! She looked at him and he winked at her. Why, he wasn't mad about the noise. He was having fun, and so was Mrs. Manley.

Janie made her thumb and finger into a circle and smiled at them.

8: Apply

## Think about the selection

1. Which of these things happened first? second? last?
   a. The animals got excited and made lots of noise.
   b. Mr. and Mrs. Manley began awarding prizes again.
   c. Janie wanted to have a pet show.
2. Why did Sarah's bird fly out of its cage?
3. What is the root word in each of the following words?

   rabbits    shaking    quietly
   flopped    asked      prizes

## Checkpoint 18

1. What was the story problem?
2. What was the solution?
3. Do you think the solution was a good one? Why or why not?
4. How did Janie feel when the animals began to run wild?
5. After the animals were quiet again, Mr. and Mrs. Manley gave out more prizes. What kind of prizes were they? Do you think the Manleys were having a good time? Why do you think as you do?

# Send Wendell

by Genevieve Gray

Wendell was six years old. He lived with Mama, Papa, William, Alice, James, Julie, Walter, and Anthony, the baby. Mama and Papa and the children all liked each other and everybody laughed most of the time.

But even when a family is happy, there is always work to do. Mama and Papa couldn't do it all alone.

"William," Papa would say, "put the clothes in the dryer for me."

But William would say, "I don't have time right now. Send Wendell." And William would hurry out.

Or Mama would say, "Alice, go over to Mrs. Turner's. Ask her if I may have a cup of sugar."

But Alice would say, "I don't have time right now. Send Wendell."

Adapted from *Send Wendell* by Genevieve Gray and Symeon Shimin. Copyright © 1974 by Genevieve Gray & Symeon Shimin. Used with permission of McGraw-Hill Book Company.

Wendell loved Mama and Papa very much and he liked to help them. His sisters and brothers did too. But sometimes Wendell wished—just a little—that the others liked to help as much as he did.

One day Wendell went to get the mail. There was a letter from Uncle Robert. "Uncle Robert is coming all the way from California to see us!" said Papa.

Wendell knew about Uncle Robert. He had a farm in California. None of the children had ever seen him, but every year he sent them birthday presents.

The days went by and the family got ready for Uncle Robert. Wendell did more to get ready than anyone else except Mama and Papa.

On one of his errands, Wendell went down to the first floor. There by the front door stood the tallest man Wendell had ever seen. The man was reading the names on all the mailboxes. Wendell stopped still and stared up at the man. And the man turned and stared at Wendell. The man began to laugh. "You must be James," he said.

"No, I'm Wendell," said Wendell, smiling.

"I'm your Uncle Robert," said the man.

Wendell and Uncle Robert hugged each other. Then Uncle Robert said, "You are going to look just like your grandfather when you grow up." Wendell felt good.

They went upstairs and everyone was very glad
to see Uncle Robert. Mama put her arms around his
neck and cried. They all talked and laughed.

That night Wendell's family had a big dinner.
Uncle Robert told about his farm in California.

When it came time for Uncle Robert to go back to California, he said, "Wendell, your Mama and Papa say when you grow up a little more you can come visit me on the farm. Would you like to do that?"

"Yes," said Wendell. He held tight to Uncle Robert's hand.

The next morning after Uncle Robert left, Mama said, "Alice, please take Mrs. Wilson's cake pan back to her."

"I don't have time," said Alice. "Send Wendell."

But Wendell smiled. "No," he said. "I can't go. I have to write a letter to Uncle Robert."

And Alice had to go anyway.

## Think about the selection

1. Why do you think Wendell was always willing to help Mama and Papa?
2. Do you think it was fair for his brothers and sisters to say, "Send Wendell"? Why or why not?
3. Why do you think Wendell held tight to Uncle Robert's hand?
4. Why do you think Wendell wouldn't take the cake pan back to Mrs. Wilson at the end of the story?
5. Do you think Uncle Robert had anything to do with Wendell wanting more time for himself? Why or why not?

# Section Two Checkpoint

## Word Identification Tests

### Subtest 1

*Which of the words below each sentence has the same vowel sound as the underlined word?*

1. Hang your coat on the <u>hook</u>.
   ⓐ grow  ⓑ wood  ⓒ cool

2. When the bear started to <u>growl</u>, the children woke up.
   ⓐ look  ⓑ thrown  ⓒ cow

3. Many of the people grew most of their <u>food</u>.
   ⓐ stool  ⓑ snow  ⓒ cook

4. Who <u>took</u> the jar of paste?
   ⓐ how  ⓑ pool  ⓒ stood

5. Karl has a <u>bowl</u> of soup.
   ⓐ frown  ⓑ low  ⓒ mouth

6. Mr. Hill owns a <u>house</u>.
   ⓐ blow  ⓑ took  ⓒ down

7. We visited a small <u>town</u>.
   ⓐ howl  ⓑ school  ⓒ slow

### Subtest 2

*What is the root word in each underlined word?*

8. The road was very <u>dusty</u>.
   ⓐ dus  ⓑ dust  ⓒ DK

9. Who was <u>driving</u> the car?
   ⓐ drive  ⓑ driv  ⓒ DK

10. The old tree was <u>leafless</u>.
    ⓐ leaf  ⓑ less  ⓒ DK

11. Ed cut the pie into <u>halves</u>.
    ⓐ have  ⓑ half  ⓒ DK

12. I was <u>hungrier</u> than Sue.
    ⓐ hung  ⓑ hungry  ⓒ DK

13. Lucy <u>hummed</u> a little tune.
    ⓐ hum  ⓑ humm  ⓒ DK

14. I don't like <u>scary</u> movies.
    ⓐ scar  ⓑ scare  ⓒ DK

15. The boy read two <u>stories</u>.
    ⓐ story  ⓑ store  ⓒ DK

240

## Subtest 3

*Turn to page 179 in your book. Find the three numbered sentences. Which numbered sentence tells how each word below was divided into syllables?*

16. sec'ond
ⓐ 1    ⓑ 2    ⓒ 3    ⓓ DK

17. jun'gle
ⓐ 1    ⓑ 2    ⓒ 3    ⓓ DK

18. tur'nip
ⓐ 1    ⓑ 2    ⓒ 3    ⓓ DK

19. flick'er
ⓐ 1    ⓑ 2    ⓒ 3    ⓓ DK

20. pi'lot
ⓐ 1    ⓑ 2    ⓒ 3    ⓓ DK

21. wig'gle
ⓐ 1    ⓑ 2    ⓒ 3    ⓓ DK

22. rath'er
ⓐ 1    ⓑ 2    ⓒ 3    ⓓ DK

23. num'ber
ⓐ 1    ⓑ 2    ⓒ 3    ⓓ DK

## Subtest 4

*Read the paragraph and then follow the directions.*

The children on Oak Street had a picnic in the park. They ate their lunch at a table in the shade. Then they took a ride on the little train. They rode to the other end of the park.

*What vowel sound do you hear in the word or the accented syllable of the word?*

24. street
ⓐ long    ⓑ short    ⓒ r-controlled

25. pic'nic
ⓐ long    ⓑ short    ⓒ r-controlled

26. park
ⓐ long    ⓑ short    ⓒ r-controlled

27. ta'ble
ⓐ long    ⓑ short    ⓒ r-controlled

28. lunch
ⓐ long    ⓑ short    ⓒ r-controlled

29. end
ⓐ long    ⓑ short    ⓒ r-controlled

# Comprehension Tests

## Subtest 5

*Finish each sentence by choosing the correct meaning of the underlined word.*

1. A <u>famous</u> person is—
   ⓐ well known  ⓑ very old
   ⓒ tall and thin  ⓓ DK

2. To <u>complain</u> is to—
   ⓐ laugh loudly  ⓑ run away
   ⓒ find fault  ⓓ DK

3. A <u>slender</u> stick is—
   ⓐ very thick
   ⓑ long and thin
   ⓒ short and heavy  ⓓ DK

4. Someone who is <u>anxious</u> is—
   ⓐ happy  ⓑ friendly
   ⓒ worried  ⓓ DK

5. A <u>hoof</u> is part of a—
   ⓐ foot  ⓑ head
   ⓒ tail  ⓓ DK

6. To <u>fetch</u> means to—
   ⓐ throw  ⓑ forget
   ⓒ bring  ⓓ DK

7. A <u>dolphin</u> is—
   ⓐ an ocean  ⓑ an animal
   ⓒ a plant  ⓓ DK

## Subtest 6

*What does the underlined word in each sentence mean?*

8. By the end of clean-up day, the yard was <u>unlittered</u>.
   ⓐ covered with litter
   ⓑ not littered  ⓒ DK

9. As Sue <u>replayed</u> the record, she heard some voices she had missed the first time.
   ⓐ didn't play
   ⓑ played again  ⓒ DK

10. The porch floor was <u>repainted</u>.
    ⓐ not painted
    ⓑ painted again  ⓒ DK

11. Al said, "I'll take my shoes off after I <u>untie</u> them."
    ⓐ do the opposite of tie
    ⓑ tie again  ⓒ DK

12. After the storm, Joe had to <u>rebuild</u> the fence.
    ⓐ build again
    ⓑ do the opposite of build
    ⓒ DK

13. Only one cup was <u>unbroken</u>.
    ⓐ broken again
    ⓑ not broken  ⓒ DK

## Subtest 7

*Read the story, and answer the questions.*

Sandra and Mark named the new kittens Fee, Fi, and Fum. They knew they didn't have room to keep all three. They had friends who wanted kittens. But which one should they keep?

Sandra liked Fee best because it had such big eyes. Mark wanted to keep Fum because it was always sitting on his shoes.

They went to Grandmother for help. She asked them how they solved such problems at school.

"Well, we vote," said Mark. "But with just two we can't."

"We can put the names in a hat and draw one out," said Sandra.

So they did. And which one was picked? Yes, it was Fi!

14. What was the story problem?
ⓐ The children couldn't think of names for the kittens.
ⓑ They couldn't decide which kitten to keep.
ⓒ They couldn't find anyone who wanted kittens.

15. How was the problem solved?
ⓐ They drew a name from a hat.
ⓑ They gave all the kittens away.
ⓒ They kept two kittens.

16. Why do you think Grandmother didn't tell the children what to do?
ⓐ She didn't know how to help.
ⓑ She wanted them to figure out a way by themselves.
ⓒ She hoped they would keep all of the kittens.

17. Why couldn't they vote?
ⓐ They couldn't find a hat.
ⓑ They didn't know how.
ⓒ There might be a tie.

## Subtest 8

18. Why did Mark like Fum best?
ⓐ It had big eyes.
ⓑ It liked Grandmother.
ⓒ It sat on his shoes.

19. Why couldn't the children keep all of the kittens?
ⓐ They put the names in a hat.
ⓑ There wasn't enough room.
ⓒ Grandmother wanted them.

## Subtest 9

Four children who lived near the ocean decided to collect seashells. The bar graph below shows how many shells each child collected. Use the graph to answer the questions.

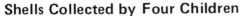

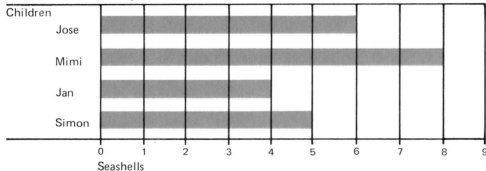

1. What do the numbers at the bottom of the graph tell you?
   ⓐ the children's names
   ⓑ the number of shells
   ⓒ the number of children
   ⓓ DK

2. How many shells did Simon collect?
   ⓐ 5    ⓑ 6    ⓒ 7    ⓓ DK

3. How many shells did Jose and Jan together find?
   ⓐ 9    ⓑ 10    ⓒ 11    ⓓ DK

4. On the first day Mimi found three shells. How many shells did she find altogether?
   ⓐ 7    ⓑ 8    ⓒ 9    ⓓ DK

5. Who collected fewer shells than Simon?
   ⓐ Jan      ⓑ Mimi
   ⓒ Jose     ⓓ DK

6. Who collected more shells than Jose?
   ⓐ Simon    ⓑ Jan
   ⓒ Mimi     ⓓ DK

Possible Study and Research Score: 6

# POOH GOES VISITING

by A. A. Milne

Edward Bear, known to his friends as
Winnie-the-Pooh, or Pooh for short, was walking
through the Forest one day, humming proudly to
himself. He had made up a little hum that very
morning, as he was doing his Stoutness Exercises
in front of the glass.

*Tra-la-la, tra-la-la,* as he stretched up as high as he
could go, and then *Tra-la-la, tra-la—oh, help!—la,*
as he tried to reach his toes.

After breakfast he had said it over and over to
himself until he had learnt it off by heart, and now
he was humming it right through, properly. It went
like this:

*Tra-la-la, tra-la-la,*
*Tra-la-la, tra-la-la,*
*Rum-tum-tiddle-um-tum.*
*Tiddle-iddle, tiddle-iddle,*
*Tiddle-iddle, tiddle-iddle,*
*Rum-tum-tum-tiddle-um.*

Well, he was humming this hum to himself, and walking along gaily, wondering what everybody else was doing, and what it felt like being somebody else, when suddenly he came to a sandy bank, and in the bank was a large hole.

"Aha!" said Pooh. "*Rum-tum-tiddle-um-tum.* If I know anything about anything, that hole means Rabbit," he said, "and Rabbit means Company," he said, "and Company means Food and Listening-to-Me-Humming and such like. *Rum-tum-tum-tiddle-um.*"

So he bent down, put his head into the hole, and called out, "Is anybody at home?"

There was a sudden scuffling noise from inside the hole, and then silence.

"What I said was, 'Is anybody at home?'" called out Pooh very loudly.

"No!" said a voice, and then added, "You needn't shout so loud. I heard you quite well the first time."

"Bother!" said Pooh. "Isn't there anybody here at all?"

"Nobody."

Winnie-the-Pooh took his head out of the hole and thought for a little, and he thought to himself, "There must be somebody there, because somebody must have *said,* 'Nobody.'" So he put his head back in the hole and said, "Hallo, Rabbit, isn't that you?"

"No," said Rabbit, in a different sort of voice this time.

"But isn't that Rabbit's voice?"

"I don't *think* so," said Rabbit. "It isn't *meant* to be."

"Oh!" said Pooh.

He took his head out of the hole and had another think, and then he put it back and said, "Well, could you very kindly tell me where Rabbit is?"

"He has gone to see his friend Pooh Bear, who is a great friend of his."

"But this *is* Me!" said Bear, very much surprised.

"What sort of Me?"

"Pooh Bear."

"Are you sure?" said Rabbit, still more surprised.

"Quite, quite sure," said Pooh.

"Oh, well, then, come in."

So Pooh pushed and pushed and pushed his way through the hole, and at last he got in.

"You were quite right," said Rabbit, looking at him all over. "It *is* you. Glad to see you."

"Who did you think it was?"

"Well, I wasn't sure. You know how it is in the Forest. One can't have *anybody* coming into one's house. One has to be *careful*. What about a mouthful of something?"

Pooh always liked a little something at eleven o'clock in the morning, and he was very glad to see Rabbit getting out the plates and mugs; and when Rabbit said, "Honey or condensed milk with your bread?" he was so excited that he said, "Both," and then, so as not to seem greedy, he added, "But don't bother about the bread, please." And for a long time after that he said nothing . . . until at last, humming to himself in a rather sticky voice, he got up, shook Rabbit lovingly by the paw, and said that he must be going on.

"Must you?" said Rabbit politely.

"Well," said Pooh, "I could stay a little longer if it —if you—" and he tried very hard to look in the direction of the larder.

"As a matter of fact," said Rabbit, "I was going out myself directly."

"Oh, well, then, I'll be going on. Good-bye."

"Well, good-bye, if you're sure you won't have any more."

"*Is* there any more?" asked Pooh quickly.

Rabbit took the covers off the dishes and said, "No, there wasn't."

"I thought not," said Pooh, nodding to himself. "Well, good-bye. I must be going on."

So he started to climb out of the hole. He pulled with his front paws and pushed with his back paws, and in a little while his nose was out in the open again . . . and then his ears . . . and then his front paws . . . and then his shoulders . . . and then—

"Oh, help!" said Pooh. "I'd better go back."

"Oh, bother!" said Pooh. "I shall have to go on."

"I can't do either!" said Pooh. "Oh, help *and* bother!"

Now by this time Rabbit wanted to go for a walk too, and finding the front door full, he went out by the back door, and came round to Pooh, and looked at him.

"Hallo, are you stuck?" he asked.

"N-no," said Pooh carelessly. "Just resting and thinking and humming to myself."

"Here, give us a paw."

Pooh Bear stretched out a paw, and Rabbit pulled and pulled and pulled. . . .

"*Ow!*" cried Pooh. "You're hurting!"

"The fact is," said Rabbit, "you're stuck."

"It all comes," said Pooh crossly, "of not having front doors big enough."

"It all comes," said Rabbit sternly, "of eating too much. I thought at the time," said Rabbit, "only I didn't like to say anything," said Rabbit, "that one of us was eating too much," said Rabbit, "and I knew it wasn't *me,*" he said. "Well, well, I shall go and fetch Christopher Robin."

Christopher Robin lived at the other end of the Forest, and when he came back with Rabbit and saw the front half of Pooh, he said, "Silly old Bear," in such a loving voice that everybody felt quite hopeful again.

"I was just beginning to think," said Bear sniffing slightly, "that Rabbit might never be able to use his front door again. And I should *hate* that," he said.

"So should I," said Rabbit.

"Use his front door again?" said Christopher Robin. "Of course he'll use his front door again."

"Good," said Rabbit.

"If we can't pull you out, Pooh, we might push you back."

Rabbit scratched his whiskers thoughtfully and pointed out that, when Pooh was pushed back, he was back, and of course nobody was more glad to see Pooh than *he* was, still there it was, some lived in trees and some lived underground and—

"You mean I'd *never* get out?" said Pooh.

"I mean," said Rabbit, "that having got <u>so</u> far, it seems a pity to waste it."

Christopher Robin nodded. "Then there's only one thing to be done," he said. "We shall have to wait for you to get thin again."

"How long does getting thin take?" asked Pooh anxiously.

"About a week, I should think."

"But I can't stay here for a *week!*"

"You can *stay* here all right, silly old Bear. It's getting you out which is so difficult."

"We'll read to you," said Rabbit cheerfully. "And I hope it won't snow," he added. "And I say, old fellow, you're taking up a good deal of room in my house—*do* you mind if I use your back legs as a towel-horse? Because, I mean, there they are—doing nothing—and it would be very convenient just to hang the towels on them."

"A week!" said Pooh gloomily. *"What about meals?"*

"I'm afraid no meals," said Christopher Robin, "because of getting thin quicker. But we *will* read to you."

Bear began to sigh, and then found he couldn't because he was so tightly stuck; and a tear rolled down his eye as he said, "Then would you read a Sustaining Book, such as would help and comfort a Wedged Bear in Great Tightness?"

So for a week Christopher Robin read that sort of book at the North end of Pooh, and Rabbit hung his washing on the South end . . . and in between Bear felt himself getting slenderer and slenderer.

And at the end of the week Christopher Robin
said, *"Now!"* So he took hold of Pooh's front
paws, and Rabbit took hold of Christopher Robin,
and all Rabbit's friends and relations took hold of
Rabbit, and they all pulled together. . . .

And for a long time Pooh only said, *"Ow!"* . . .
And *"Oh!"*

And then, all of a sudden, he said, *"Pop!"* just as if a cork were coming out of a bottle.

And Christopher Robin and Rabbit and all Rabbit's friends and relations went head-over-heels backwards . . . and on top of them came Winnie-the-Pooh—free!

So, with a nod of thanks to his friends, he went on with his walk through the Forest, humming proudly to himself. But Christopher Robin looked after him lovingly, and said to himself, "Silly old Bear!"

# Glossary

## Full Pronunciation Key

The pronunciation of each word is shown just after the word, in this way:
**ab bre vi ate** (ə brē′vē āt).

The letters and signs used are pronounced as in the words below.

The mark ′ is placed after a syllable with primary or heavy accent, as in the example above.

The mark ′ after a syllable shows a secondary or lighter accent, as in
**ab bre vi a tion** (ə brē′vē ā′shən).

| | | | | | | | |
|---|---|---|---|---|---|---|---|
| **a** | hat, cap | **j** | jam, enjoy | | **u** | cup, butter |
| **ā** | age, face | **k** | kind, seek | | **u̇** | full, put |
| **ä** | father, far | **l** | land, coal | | **ü** | rule, move |
| | | **m** | me, am | | | |
| **b** | bad, rob | **n** | no, in | | **v** | very, save |
| **ch** | child, much | **ng** | long, bring | | **w** | will, woman |
| **d** | did, red | | | | **y** | young, yet |
| | | **o** | hot, rock | | **z** | zero, breeze |
| **e** | let, best | **ō** | open, go | | **zh** | measure, seizure |
| **ē** | equal, be | **ô** | order, all | | | |
| **ėr** | term, learn | **oi** | oil, voice | | | |
| | | **ou** | house, out | | **ə** | represents: |
| **f** | fat, if | | | | | a in about |
| **g** | go, bag | **p** | paper, cup | | | e in taken |
| **h** | he, how | **r** | run, try | | | i in pencil |
| | | **s** | say, yes | | | o in lemon |
| **i** | it, pin | **sh** | she, rush | | | u in circus |
| **ī** | ice, five | **t** | tell, it | | | |
| | | **th** | thin, both | | | |
| | | **ᴛʜ** | then, smooth | | | |

The contents of the Glossary entries in this book have been adapted from *Scott, Foresman Beginning Dictionary,* Copyright © 1976 by Scott, Foresman and Company and *My Second Picture Dictionary,* by William A. Jenkins and Andrew Schiller, Copyright © 1975, 1971 by Scott, Foresman and Company.

259

# A a

**aisle** (īl), **1** passage between rows of seats in a hall, theater, church, or school. **2** any long, narrow passage. *noun.*

**anx ious** (angk'shəs), **1** uneasy because of thoughts or fears of what may happen; troubled; worried: *I felt anxious about my final exams. The week of the flood was an anxious time for all of us.* **2** wishing very much; eager. *adjective.*

**a part** (ə pärt'), **1** to pieces; in pieces; in separate parts: *She took the watch apart to see how it runs.* **2** away from each other: *Keep the dogs apart.* **3** to one side; aside: *He sets some money apart for a vacation each year. adverb.*

**ap pear** (ə pir'), **1** be seen; come in sight: *One by one the stars appear.* **2** seem; look: *The apple appeared sound on the outside, but it was rotten inside. verb.*

**a quar i um** (ə kwer'ē əm), **1** tank or glass bowl in which living fish, other water animals, and water plants are kept. See picture. **2** building used for showing collections of living fish, water animals, and water plants. *noun.*

aquarium (definition 1)

# B b

**bat¹** (bat), **1** a stout wooden stick or club, used to hit the ball in baseball, cricket, and similar games. **2** hit with a bat; hit: *He bats well. I batted the balloon with my hand.* **3** a turn at batting: *Who goes to bat first?* **1,3** *noun,* **2** *verb,* **bat ted, bat ting.**

**bat²** (bat), a flying mammal with a body like that of a mouse and wings made of thin skin. Bats fly at night. Most of them eat insects but some live on fruit and a few suck the blood of other mammals. See picture. *noun.*

bat²—wingspread about 15 inches (38 centimeters)

**be gin ning** (bi gin'ing), **1** a start: *to make a good beginning.* **2** time when anything begins: *December 22nd marks the beginning of winter.* **3** first part: *I enjoyed this book from beginning to end. noun.*

**be neath** (bi nēth'), **1** in a lower place; below; underneath; under: *What you drop will fall upon the spot beneath. The dog sat beneath the tree.* **2** not worthy of: *Your insulting remarks are beneath notice.* **1** *adverb,* **1,2** *preposition.*

**boar** (bôr), **1** a male pig or hog. **2** a wild pig or hog. See picture. *noun.*

boar (definition 2)
2¹/₂ feet (76 centimeters) high at the shoulder

**breathe** (brēᴛʜ), **1** draw air into the lungs and force it out. You breathe through your nose or through your mouth. **2** stop for breath; stop to rest after hard work or exercise: *Let's take a minute to breathe before we begin to work again.* **3** say softly; whisper: *Don't breathe a word of this to anyone. verb,* **breathed, breath ing.**

# C c

**calf**[1] (kaf), **1** a young cow or bull. **2** a young deer, elephant, whale, or seal. *noun, plural* **calves.**

**calf**[2] (kaf), the thick, fleshy part of the back of the leg below the knee. *noun, plural* **calves.**

**cap tain** (cap′tən), **1** head of a group; leader or chief: *the captain of a basketball team.* **2** commander of a ship. **3** an army, air force, or marine officer ranking below a major. **4** lead or command as captain: *She will captain the softball team next season.* 1-3 *noun,* 4 *verb.*

| **a** hat | **i** it | **oi** oil | **ch** child | a in about |
|---|---|---|---|---|
| **ā** age | **ī** ice | **ou** out | **ng** long | e in taken |
| **ä** far | **o** hot | **u** cup | **sh** she  ə = | i in pencil |
| **e** let | **ō** open | **ù** put | **th** thin | o in lemon |
| **ē** equal | **ô** order | **ü** rule | **ᴛʜ** then | u in circus |
| **ėr** term | | | **zh** measure | |

**care ful** (ker′fəl *or* kar′fəl), **1** thinking what one says; watching what one does; watchful; cautious: *He is careful to tell the truth at all times. Be careful with my new bicycle!* **2** showing care; done with thought or effort; exact; thorough: *Arithmetic requires careful work. adjective.*

**care less** (ker′lis *or* kar′lis), **1** not thinking or watching what you say or do; not careful: *I was careless and broke the cup.* **2** done without enough thought or effort; not exact or thorough: *careless work.* **3** not caring or troubling; indifferent: *a careless attitude toward school. adjective.*

**catch** (kach), **1** take and hold (something moving); seize: *Catch the ball with both hands. The children chased the puppy and caught it.* **2** take or get: *Paper catches fire easily. Put on a warm coat or you will catch cold. I caught a glimpse of my grandmother waving as her plane took off.* **3** reach or get to in time: *You have just five minutes to catch your train.* **4** see, hear, or understand: *He spoke so rapidly that I didn't catch the meaning of what he said.* **5** become hooked or fastened: *My sweater caught in the door.* **6** come upon suddenly; surprise: *Mother caught me just as I was hiding her birthday present.* **7** act as catcher in baseball: *He catches for our team.* **8** act of catching: *She made a fine catch with one hand.* **9** thing that fastens: *The catch on that door is broken.* **10** thing caught: *A dozen fish is a good catch.* 1-7 *verb,* **caught, catch ing;** 8-10 *noun, plural* **catch es.**

**char ac ter** (kar′ik tər), **1** all the qualities or features of anything; kind; sort; nature: *The soil on the prairies is of a different character from that in the mountains.* **2** moral nature; moral strength or weakness. The special way in which you feel, think, and act, considered as good or bad, makes up your character. *She has an honest, dependable character.* **3** person or animal in a play, poem, story, or book: *My favorite character in "Charlotte's Web" is Wilbur, the pig. noun.*

**chill** (chil), **1** unpleasant coldness: *There's a chill in the air today.* **2** unpleasantly cold: *A chill wind blew across the lake.* **3** make or become cold: *The icy wind chilled us to the bone. My blood chilled as I read the horror story.* **4** a sudden coldness of the body with shivering: *I had a chill yesterday and still feel ill.* 1,4 *noun*, 2 *adjective*, 3 *verb*.

**chill y** (chil´ē), **1** cold; unpleasantly cool: *It is a rainy, chilly day.* **2** cold in manner; unfriendly: *We gave a chilly reception to the people who came to our party uninvited. adjective*, **chill i er, chill i est.**

**coat** (kōt), **1** outer garment of cloth or fur with sleeves: *a winter coat. Father wears a coat and tie to work.* **2** any outer covering: *a dog's coat of hair. noun.*

**com fort** (kum´fərt), **1** ease the grief or sorrow of. See picture. **2** anything that makes trouble or sorrow easier to bear: *Your friendship brought me comfort while I was sick.* **3** person or thing that makes life easier or takes away hardship: *the warm fire was a comfort to the cold campers.* **4** ease; freedom from hardship: *It's nice to have enough money to live in comfort.* 1 *verb*, 2-4 *noun*.

comfort (definition 1)
The police officer comforted the frightened child.

**com fort a ble** (kum´fər tə bəl), **1** giving comfort: *A soft, warm bed is comfortable.* **2** in comfort; free from pain or hardship: *We felt comfortable in the warm house after a cold day outdoors. adjective.*

**com plain** (kəm plān´), **1** say that something is wrong; find fault: *We complained that the room was cold.* **2** talk about one's pain or troubles: *He is always complaining about his health.* **3** make an accusation or charge: *I complained to the police about the barking of my neighbor's dog. verb.*

**con clu sion** (kən klü´zhən), **1** end: *the conclusion of the story.* Textbooks sometimes have conclusions summing up all the important facts in a chapter. **2** decision or opinion reached by reasoning: *She came to the conclusion that she would have to work harder to finish on time. noun.*

**con dense** (kən dens´), **1** make denser; become more compact: *Milk is condensed by removing much of the water from it.* **2** increase the strength of: *Light is condensed by means of lenses. verb*, **con densed, con dens ing.**

**con trol** (kən trōl´), **1** have power or authority over; direct: *The government controls the printing of money.* **2** power; authority; direction: *Children are under their parents' control.* **3** hold back; keep down: *I was so upset by the accident that I couldn't control my tears.* **4** a holding back; a keeping down; restraint; check: *to lose control of one's temper.* 1,3 *verb*, **con trolled, con trol ling;** 2,4 *noun*.

**con ven ient** (kən vē´nyənt), **1** suitable; saving trouble; well arranged; easy to use: *take a convenient bus, live in a convenient house.* **2** easily done; not troublesome: *Will it be convenient for you to bring your lunch to school?* **3** within easy reach; handy: *meet at a convenient place. adjective.*

**cot** (kot), narrow bed, sometimes made of canvas stretched on a frame that folds together. *noun.*

**cross** (krôs), **1** stick or post with another across it like a T or an X. **2** draw a line across: *In writing you cross the letter "t." She crossed out the wrong word.* **3** put or lay across: *He crossed his arms.* **4** move from one side to another; go across: *He crossed the street. The bridge crosses the river.* **5** lying or going across; crossing: *I saw you standing at the intersection of the cross streets.* **6** act against; get in the way of; oppose: *If anyone crosses him, he gets very angry.* **7** in a bad temper: *Children are often cross when they don't feel well.* 1 *noun*, plural **cross es;** 2-4,6 *verb*, 5,7 *adjective*.

**cup board** (kub'ərd), closet or cabinet with shelves for dishes and food supplies. See picture. *noun.*

cupboard

# D d

**dare** (der *or* dar), **1** be bold; be bold enough: *The children dared to explore the haunted house.* **2** have courage to try; be bold enough for; not be afraid of: *The pioneers dared the dangers of a strange land.* **3** challenge: *I dare you to jump the puddle.* **4** a challenge: *I took his dare to jump.* 1-3 *verb,* **dared, dar ing;** 4 *noun.*

**dar ing** (der'ing *or* dar'ing), **1** boldness; courage to take risks: *The lifeguard's daring saved a swimmer's life.* **2** bold; fearless: *Saving the swimmer was a daring act.* 1 *noun,* 2 *adjective.*

| **a** hat | **i** it | **oi** oil | **ch** child | a in about |
|---|---|---|---|---|
| **ā** age | **ī** ice | **ou** out | **ng** long | e in taken |
| **ä** far | **o** hot | **u** cup | **sh** she | ə = i in pencil |
| **e** let | **ō** open | **ù** put | **th** thin | o in lemon |
| **ē** equal | **ô** order | **ü** rule | **ŦH** then | u in circus |
| **ėr** term | | | **zh** measure | |

**dash** (dash), **1** throw: *In a fit of anger he dashed his ruler against the door.* **2** splash: *The car sped by and dashed muddy water all over me.* **3** a splash: *She was sprayed by a dash of salt water.* **4** to rush: *They dashed by in a hurry.* **5** a rush: *She made a dash for safety.* **6** throw and break; smash: *I was so angry I dashed the glass to bits on the tile floor.* **7** ruin: *Our hopes were dashed by the bad news.* **8** small amount: *Put in just a dash of pepper.* **9** a short race: *the fifty-yard dash.* 1,2,4,6,7 *verb,* 3,5,8,9 *noun.*

**den** (den), **1** a wild animal's home: *The bear's den was in a cave.* **2** place where thieves or the like have their headquarters. **3** one's private room for reading and work, usually small and cozy. *noun.*

**de scribe** (di skrīb'), **1** tell in words how a person looks, feels, or acts, or how a place, a thing, or an event looks; tell or write about: *The reporter described the accident in detail.* **2** trace or form; draw the outline of: *The spinning top described a figure 8.* *verb,* **de scribed, de scrib ing.**

**des ert** (dez'ərt), **1** region without water and trees. It is usually sandy. There is a great desert in the northern part of Africa. **2** not inhabited or cultivated; wild: *They were shipwrecked on a desert island.* 1 *noun,* 2 *adjective.*

**di rect ly** (də rekt'lē), **1** in a direct line or manner; straight: *This road runs directly into the center of town.* **2** exactly; absolutely: *directly opposite.* **3** immediately; at once: *Come home directly.* *adverb.*

**dis grace** (dis grās'), **1** loss of honor or respect; shame: *The disgrace of being sent to prison was hard for them to bear.* **2** loss of favor or trust: *The king's former adviser is now in disgrace.* **3** cause disgrace to; bring shame upon: *The traitor disgraced his family and friends.* **4** person or thing that causes dishonor or shame: *The slums in many cities are a disgrace.* 1,2,4 *noun,* 3 *verb,* **dis graced, dis grac ing.**

**dol phin** (dol′fən), a sea mammal much like a small whale. It has a snout like a beak and remarkable intelligence. See picture. *noun.*

dolphin—about 10 feet long (3 meters)

**es cape** (e skāp′), **1** get free; get out and away: *The bird escaped from its cage.* **2** keep free or safe from: *We all escaped the measles.* **3** act of escaping: *Their escape was aided by the thick fog.* **4** way of escaping: *There was no escape from the trap.* 1,2 *verb,* **es caped, es cap ing;** 3,4 *noun.*

**es pe cial ly** (e spesh′ə lē), more than others; particularly; principally; chiefly: *This book is especially designed for students. adverb.*

**ex pect** (ek spekt′), **1** look for; think something will probably come or happen: *We expect hot days in summer.* **2** think; suppose; guess: *I expect you're right about that. verb.*

# E e

**el e va tor** (el′ə vā′tər), **1** something which raises or lifts up. **2** a moving platform or cage to carry people and things up and down in a building or mine. *noun.*

**emp ty** (emp′tē), **1** with nothing in it: *The birds had gone, and their nest was left empty.* **2** pour out or take out all that is in (a thing): *He emptied his glass quickly.* **3** flow out: *The Mississippi River empties into the Gulf of Mexico.* 1 *adjective,* **emp ti er, emp ti est;** 2,3 *verb,* **emp tied, emp ty ing.**

**end less** (end′lis), **1** having no end; never stopping; lasting or going on forever: *the endless rotation of the earth around the sun.* **2** seeming to have no end: *Doing housework is an endless task.* **3** joined in a circle; without ends: *The chain that turns the back wheel of a bicycle is an endless chain. adjective.*

**er rand** (er′ənd), **1** trip to do something: *She has gone on an errand to the store.* **2** what one is sent to do: *I did ten errands in one trip. noun.*

**es ca la tor** (es′kə lā′tər), a moving stairway: *The store had both an elevator and an escalator. noun.*

# F f

**fa mous** (fā′məs), very well known; noted: *The famous singer was greeted by a large crowd. adjective.*

**fetch** (fech), go and get; bring: *Please fetch me my glasses. verb.*

**flap** (flap), **1** swing or sway about loosely and with some noise: *The sails flapped in the wind.* **2** move (wings or arms) up and down: *The goose flapped its wings but could not rise from the ground.* **3** fly by flapping the wings: *The bird flapped away.* **4** a flapping motion; flapping noise: *the flap of banners, the flap of a bird's wing.* **5** strike noisily with something broad and flat: *The clown's big shoes flapped along the ground.* **6** piece hanging or fastened at one edge only: *a coat with flaps on the pockets.* 1-3,5 *verb,* **flapped, flap ping;** 4,6 *noun.*

**flop** (flop), **1** move loosely or heavily; flap around clumsily: *The fish flopped helplessly on the deck.* **2** fall, drop, throw, or move heavily or clumsily: *The tired girl flopped down into a chair.* **3** flopping: *I threw myself on the bed with a flop.* **4** a dull, heavy sound made by flopping. **5** failure: *The party was a flop.* **6** fail: *Their first business venture flopped.* 1,2,6 *verb,* **flopped, flop ping;** 3-5 *noun.*

**fluff** (fluf), **1** soft, light, downy particles, such as hair, tiny feathers, or bits of wool. **2** a soft, light, downy mass: *The kitten looked like a fluff of fur.* **3** puff out into a soft, light mass. 1,2 *noun,* 3 *verb.*

**fly¹** (flī), **1** any of a large group of insects that have two wings, including houseflies, mosquitoes, and gnats. There are many different kinds of flies. **2** fishhook with feathers, silk, or tinsel on it to make it look like a fly. See picture. *noun, plural* **flies.**

fly¹ (definition 2)—The shape and movement of these flies in the water attract fish.

**fly²** (flī), **1** move through the air with wings: *These birds fly long distances.* **2** float or wave in the air: *Our flag flies every day.* **3** cause to float or wave in the air: *The children are flying kites.* **4** travel in an aircraft: *He flew to Hawaii for a vacation.* **5** pilot (an aircraft): *My cousin flies for an airline. He flies planes for a living.* **6** carry by aircraft: *The government flew food and other supplies to the flooded city.* **7** baseball hit high in the air with a bat. **8** bat a baseball high in the air. 1-6,8 *verb,* **flew, flown, fly ing** for 1-6, **flied, fly ing** for 8; 7 *noun, plural* **flies.**

| | | | | |
|---|---|---|---|---|
| **a** hat | **i** it | **oi** oil | **ch** child | a in about |
| **ā** age | **ī** ice | **ou** out | **ng** long | e in taken |
| **ä** far | **o** hot | **u** cup | **sh** she | ə = i in pencil |
| **e** let | **ō** open | **ù** put | **th** thin | o in lemon |
| **ē** equal | **ô** order | **ü** rule | **ŦH** then | u in circus |
| **ėr** term | | | **zh** measure | |

# G g

**gai ly** (gā′lē), **1** in a happy way; merrily; happily; in a gay manner. **2** brightly: *They were gaily dressed in colorful costumes. adverb.*

**gay** (gā), **1** happy and full of fun; merry: *The children were cheerful and gay on the day of the first snowfall.* **2** bright-colored: *a gay dress. adjective.*

**ger bil** (jėr′bəl), an animal somewhat like a mouse with long hind legs. Gerbils are used for scientific experiments and are kept as pets. *noun.*

**glass** (glas), **1** a hard substance that breaks easily and can usually be seen through. Windows are made of glass. **2** something to drink from made of glass: *He filled the glass with water.* **3** amount a glass can hold: *Drink a glass of water.* **4** mirror: *Look at yourself in the glass.* **5 glasses,** pair of glass lenses to help vision. **6** lens, telescope, or other thing made of glass. **7** made of glass: *a glass dish.* **8** cover or protect with glass. 1-6 *noun, plural* **glass es;** 7 *adjective,* 8 *verb.*

**gold** (gōld), **1** a heavy, bright-yellow, precious metal. Gold is used in making coins, watches, and rings. **2** made of this metal: *a gold watch.* **3** money in large sums; wealth; riches. **4** bright yellow. 1,3 *noun,* 2,4 *adjective.*

**gold en** (gōl′dən), **1** made of or containing gold. **2** shining like gold; bright-yellow: *golden hair.* **3** very good; extremely favorable, valuable, or important: *a golden opportunity.* **4** very happy; flourishing: *a golden age. adjective.*

**greed** (grēd), wanting more than one's share; greedy behavior; greedy desire: *a miser's greed for money. noun.*

**greed i ly** (grē′dl ē), in a greedy manner. *adverb.*

**greed y** (grē′dē), **1** wanting to get more than one's share; wanting to get a great deal: *The dictator was greedy for power and money. The lonely child was greedy for affection.* **2** wanting to eat a great deal in a hurry. *adjective,* **greed i er, greed i est.**

**grown-up** (grōn′up), **1** arrived at full growth; adult: *a grown-up person, grown-up manners.* **2** an adult: *The children conducted themselves like grown-ups.* **1** *adjective,* **2** *noun.*

**gulp** (gulp), **1** swallow eagerly or greedily: *The hungry girl gulped down the bowl of soup.* **2** act of swallowing: *He ate the cookie in one gulp.* **3** amount swallowed at one time; mouthful: *She took a gulp of milk.* **1** *verb,* **2,3** *noun.*

# H h

**hand ker chief** (hang′kər chif), a soft square of cloth used for wiping the nose, face, or hands. *noun.*

**hare** (her *or* har), animal with long ears, a divided upper lip, a short tail, and long hind legs. A hare is very much like a rabbit, but larger. *noun, plural* **hares** *or* **hare.**

**harp** (härp), a large stringed musical instrument played with the fingers. *noun.*

**hedge hog** (hej′hog′), **1** a small animal of Europe, Asia, and Africa, with spines on its back. When attacked, hedgehogs roll up into a bristling ball. **2** porcupine of North America. *noun.*

**hike** (hīk), **1** take a long walk; tramp; march. **2** a long walk; tramp or march: *It was a four-mile hike through the forest to the camp.* **1** *verb,* **hiked, hik ing;** **2** *noun.*

**hock ey** (hok′ē), game played by two teams on ice or on a field. The players hit a rubber disk or a ball with curved sticks to drive it across a goal. *noun.*

**hol low** (hol′ō), having nothing, or only air, inside; empty; with a hole inside; not solid: *A tube or pipe is hollow. Most rubber balls are hollow. adjective.*

**hoof** (huf), **1** a hard, horny covering on the feet of horses, cattle, sheep, pigs, and some other animals. **2** the whole foot of such animals. *noun, plural* **hoofs** *or* **hooves.**

**hoofed** (huft), having hoofs. *adjective.*

# I i

**i mag ine** (i maj′ən), form a picture of in the mind; have an idea: *The girl likes to imagine herself a doctor. We can hardly imagine life without electricity. verb,* **i mag ined, i mag in ing.**

**in for ma tion** (in′fər mā′shən), **1** knowledge given or received of some fact or circumstance; news: *We have just received information of the astronauts' safe landing.* **2** things known; facts: *A dictionary contains much information about words. noun.*

# L l

**lar der** (lär′dər), **1** pantry; place where food is kept. **2** stock of food: *The hunter's larder included flour, bacon, and deer meat. noun.*

**lit ter** (lit′ər), **1** little bits left about in disorder; things scattered about: *We picked up the litter.* **2** scatter things about; leave odds and ends lying around; make untidy: *You have littered the room with your papers.* **3** the young animals produced at one time: *a litter of puppies.* **1,3** *noun,* **2** *verb.*

**lone ly** (lōn′lē), **1** feeling oneself alone and longing for company or friends: *He was lonely while his brother was away.* **2** without many people: *a lonely road.* **3** alone: *a lonely tree. adjective,* **lone li er, lone li est.**

| | | | | |
|---|---|---|---|---|
| **a** hat | **i** it | **oi** oil | **ch** child | a in about |
| **ā** age | **ī** ice | **ou** out | **ng** long | e in taken |
| **ä** far | **o** hot | **u** cup | **sh** she ə = | i in pencil |
| **e** let | **ō** open | **u̇** put | **th** thin | o in lemon |
| **ē** equal | **ô** order | **ü** rule | **ᴛʜ** then | u in circus |
| **ėr** term | | | **zh** measure | |

# M m

**mane** (mān), the long, heavy hair on the back of or around the neck of a horse or a lion. See picture. *noun.*

mane

**match¹** (mach), **1** a short, slender piece of wood or pasteboard tipped with a mixture that takes fire when rubbed on a rough or specially prepared surface. **2** wick or cord prepared to burn at a uniform rate, for firing guns and cannon. *noun, plural* **match es.**

**match²** (mach), **1** an equal; person or thing equal to another or much like another: *A child is not a match for an adult.* **2** be equal to in a contest: *No one could match the skill of the unknown archer.* **3** two persons or things that are alike or go well together: *Those two horses make a good match.* **4** be alike; go well together: *The rugs and the wallpaper match.* **5** find the equal of or one exactly like: *Until I can match this wool, I won't be able to finish knitting the sweater.* **6** game; contest: *a boxing match, a tennis match.* **7** try (one's skill or strength against); oppose: *She matched her skill against mine.* **1,3,6** *noun, plural* **match es; 2,4,5,7** *verb.*

**mes sage** (mes′ij), **1** words sent from one person to another: *a radio message, a message of welcome.* **2** an official speech or writing: *the President's message to Congress. noun.*

**mo las ses** (mə las′iz), a sweet, brown syrup. Molasses is obtained in the process of making sugar from sugar cane. *noun.*

**mouth ful** (mouth′fu̇l), **1** the amount the mouth can easily hold. **2** what is taken into the mouth at one time. **3** a small amount. *noun, plural* **mouth fuls.**

**mug** (mug), **1** a heavy china or metal drinking cup with a handle. **2** amount a mug holds: *drink a mug of milk. noun.*

# N n

**naugh ty** (nô′tē), bad; not behaving well: *The naughty child hit his baby brother. adjective,* **naugh ti er, naugh ti est.**

**neigh bor** (nā′bər), **1** someone who lives in the next house or nearby. **2** a person or thing that is near or next to another: *The big tree brought down several of its smaller neighbors as it fell.* **3** live or be near to. **1,2** *noun,* **3** *verb.*

**neigh bor hood** (nā′bər hu̇d), **1** region near some place or thing: *She lives in the neighborhood of the mill.* **2** place; district: *Is North Street in a good neighborhood?* **3** people living near one another; people of a place: *The whole neighborhood came to the big party.* **4** of a neighborhood: *a neighborhood newspaper.* **1-3** *noun,* **4** *adjective.*

# P p

**pec car y** (pek′ər ē), a wild animal with hoofs that is somewhat like a pig. It is found in South America and as far north as Texas. *noun, plural* **pec car ies** or **pec car y.**

**peek** (pēk), **1** look quickly and slyly; peep: *You must not peek while you are counting in hide-and-seek.* **2** a quick, sly look. **1** *verb,* **2** *noun.*

**pitch**[1] (pich), **1** throw; fling; hurl; toss: *They were pitching horseshoes.* **2** (in baseball) to throw (a ball) to the player batting. **3** act of pitching; a throw or toss: *The first pitch was a strike.* 1,2 *verb*, 3 *noun*, *plural* **pitch es.**

**pitch**[2] (pich), a black, sticky substance made from tar or turpentine, used to cover the seams of wooden ships, to cover roofs, or to make pavements. *noun*, *plural* **pitch es.**

**pit y** (pit′ē), **1** sympathy; sorrow for another's suffering or distress; feeling for the sorrows of others. **2** feel pity for: *I pitied the homeless puppy.* **3** cause for pity or regret; thing to be sorry for: *It is a pity to be kept in the house in fine weather.* 1,3 *noun*, *plural* **pit ies;** 2 *verb*, **pit ied, pit y ing.**

**poke** (pōk), **1** push against with something pointed; thrust into: *poke the ashes of a fire. He poked me in the ribs with his elbow.* **2** thrust; push: *The dog poked its head out of the car window.* **3** poking; thrust; push. **4** go in a lazy way; loiter: *She felt tired and just poked around the house all day.* 1,2,4 *verb*, **poked, pok ing;** 3 *noun*.

**pol lute** (pə lüt′), make dirty; defile: *The water at the bathing beach was polluted by refuse from the factory. verb*, **pol lut ed, pol lut ing.**

**pol lu tion** (pə lü′shən), a making dirty or impure: *Exhaust from automobiles causes air pollution. noun.*

**prob lem** (prob′ləm), **1** question; difficult question: *How to do away with poverty is a problem that concerns the government.* **2** matter of doubt or difficulty: *The president of a large company has to deal with many problems.* **3** something to be worked out: *a problem in arithmetic. noun.*

**pro tect** (prə tekt′), shield from harm or danger; shelter; defend; guard: *Protect yourself from danger. Protect the baby's eyes from the sun. verb.*

**pro tec tion** (prə tek′shən), **1** act of protecting; condition of being kept from harm; defense: *We have a large dog for our protection.* **2** thing or person that prevents damage: *A hat is a protection from the sun. noun.*

**purr** (pėr), **1** a low, murmuring sound such as a cat makes when pleased. **2** make this sound. 1 *noun*, 2 *verb*.

**puz zle** (puz′əl), **1** a hard problem: *How to get all my things into one trunk is a puzzle.* **2** problem or task to be done for fun: *A famous Chinese puzzle has seven pieces of wood to fit together.* **3** make unable to understand something; confuse: *How the cat got out puzzled us.* See picture. **4** be confused. **5** use one's mind on something hard: *They puzzled over their arithmetic for an hour.* 1,2 *noun*, 3-5 *verb*, **puz zled, puz zling.**

puzzle (definition 3)—The shape of the statue puzzled him.

# Q q

**quart** (kwôrt), **1** a unit for measuring liquids equal to one fourth of a gallon: *a quart of milk.* **2** unit for measuring dry things equal to one eighth of a peck: *a quart of berries. noun.*

# R r

| | | | | |
|---|---|---|---|---|
| **a** hat | **i** it | **oi** oil | **ch** child | a in about |
| **ā** age | **ī** ice | **ou** out | **ng** long | e in taken |
| **ä** far | **o** hot | **u** cup | **sh** she | ə = i in pencil |
| **e** let | **ō** open | **ů** put | **th** thin | o in lemon |
| **ē** equal | **ô** order | **ü** rule | **ŦH** then | u in circus |
| **ėr** term | | | **zh** measure | |

**re cess** (rē′ses *or* ri ses′ *for 1;* ri ses′ *for 2*), **1** time during which work stops: *Our school has an hour's recess at noon.* **2** take a recess: *The committee recessed for lunch.* 1 *noun,* 2 *verb.*

**rest ful** (rest′fəl), **1** full of rest; giving rest: *She had a restful nap.* **2** quiet; peaceful. *adjective.*

**root**[1] (rüt), **1** part of a plant that grows down into the soil, holds the plant in place, and absorbs food and water from the soil. **2** any underground part of a plant. **3** pull, tear, or dig (up or out) by the roots; get rid of completely. **4** word from which other words are made. *Room* is the root of *roominess, roomer, roommate,* and *roomy.* 1,2,4 *noun,* 3 *verb.*

**root**[2] (rüt), **1** dig with the snout: *The pigs rooted up the garden.* **2** rummage: *She rooted through the closet looking for her old shoes.* *verb.*

**seal**[1] (sēl), **1** design stamped on a piece of wax or other soft material, used to show ownership or authority. The seal of the United States is attached to important government papers. **2** stamp for marking things with such a design: *a seal with one's initials on it.* **3** piece of wax, paper, or metal on which the design is stamped. **4** close very tightly; fasten: *Seal the letter before mailing it. I sealed the jars of fruit. Her promise sealed her lips.* 1-3 *noun,* 4 *verb.*

**seal**[2] (sēl), **1** a sea animal with large flippers, usually living in cold regions. Some kinds have very valuable fur. **2** its fur. *noun, plural* **seals** *or* **seal.**

**shade** (shād), **1** a partly dark place, not in the sunshine: *Let's sit in the shade of that tree.* **2** a slight darkness or coolness given by something that cuts off light: *Big trees cast shade.* **3** something that shuts out light: *Pull down the shades of the windows.* **4** keep light from: *A big hat shades the eyes.* **5** lightness or darkness of color: *I want to see silks in all shades of blue.* 1-3,5 *noun,* 4 *verb,* **shad ed, shad ing.**

# S s

**sad dle** (sad′l), **1** seat for a rider on a horse's back, on a bicycle, or on other like things. See pictures. **2** put a saddle on: *Saddle the horse.* 1 *noun,* 2 *verb,* **sad dled, sad dling.**

**scuf fle** (skuf′əl), **1** struggle or fight in a rough, confused manner: *The children were scuffling over the ball.* **2** a confused, rough struggle or fight: *I lost my hat in the scuffle.* 1 *verb,* **scuf fled, scuf fling;** 2 *noun.*

saddles (definition 1)

Western saddle

English saddle

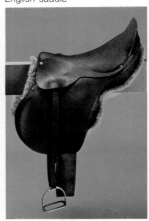

**sharp** (shärp), **1** having a thin cutting edge or a fine point: *a sharp knife.* **2** having a point; not rounded: *a sharp corner on a box.* **3** with a sudden change of direction: *a sharp turn.* **4** very cold: *sharp weather.* **5** severe; biting: *sharp words.* **6** fierce; violent: *a sharp struggle.* **7** being aware of things quickly: *sharp ears.* **8** in a sharp manner; in an alert manner; keenly: *Look sharp!* 1-7 *adjective,* 8 *adverb.*

**shield** (shēld), **1** piece of armor carried on the arm to protect the body in battle. **2** anything used to protect: *I turned up my collar as a shield against the cold wind.* **3** something shaped like a shield. **4** protect; defend: *They shielded me from unjust punishment.* 1-3 *noun,* 4 *verb.*

**shy** (shī), **1** uncomfortable in company; bashful: *He is shy and dislikes parties.* **2** easily frightened away; timid: *A deer is a shy animal. adjective,* **shy er, shy est,** or **shi er, shi est.**

**sign** (sīn), **1** any mark or thing used to mean, represent, or point out something: *The sign reads, ''Keep off the grass.'' The signs for add, subtract, multiply, and divide are* +, −, ×, *and* ÷. **2** put one's name on; write one's name. A person signs a letter, a note promising to pay a debt, or a check. We sign for telegrams or parcels. **3** motion or gesture used to mean, represent, or point out something: *A nod is a sign of agreement.* 1,3 *noun,* 2 *verb.*

**si lence** (sī′ləns), **1** absence of sound or noise; stillness: *The teacher asked for silence.* **2** keeping still; not talking: *Silence gives consent.* **3** not mentioning: *Mother passed over his foolish remarks in silence.* **4** stop the noise of; make silent; quiet: *Please silence that barking dog.* 1-3 *noun,* 4 *verb,* **si lenced, si lenc ing.**

**si lent** (sī′lənt), **1** quiet; still; noiseless: *a silent house.* **2** not speaking; saying little or nothing: *The stranger was silent about his early life. Pupils must be silent during the study hour.* **3** not spoken; not said out loud: *a silent prayer. The ''e'' in ''time'' is a silent letter.* See picture. *adjective.*

**sip** (sip), **1** drink little by little: *She sipped her tea.* **2** a very small drink: *She took a sip.* 1 *verb,* **sipped, sip ping;** 2 *noun.*

**slen der** (slen′dər), **1** long and thin; not big around; slim: *a slender child. A pencil is a slender piece of wood.* **2** slight; small: *a slender meal, a slender income, a slender hope. adjective.*

**slid** (slid). See **slide.** *The minutes slid rapidly by. She has slid past us. verb.*

**slide** (slīd), **1** move smoothly, as a sled moves on snow or ice: *The bureau drawers slide in and out.* **2** move easily, quietly, or secretly: *The thief quickly slid behind the curtains.* **3** pass or put quietly or secretly: *I slid the note into my pocket.* **4** act of sliding: *The children each take a slide in turn.* 1-3 *verb,* **slid, slid ing;** 4 *noun.*

**slip**[1] (slip), **1** go or move smoothly, quietly, easily, or quickly: *She slipped out of the room. Time slips by.* **2** slide; move out of place: *The knife slipped and cut him.* **3** slide suddenly without wanting to: *He slipped on the icy sidewalk.* **4** slipping: *My broken leg was caused by a slip on a banana peel.* 1-3 *verb,* **slipped, slip ping;** 4 *noun.*

**slip**[2] (slip), **1** a narrow strip of paper, wood, or other material. **2** a small branch or twig cut from a plant to grow a new plant: *She has promised us slips from that bush. noun.*

**slip per y** (slip′ər ē), **1** causing or likely to cause slipping: *A wet street is slippery. The steps are slippery with ice.* **2** slipping away easily: *Wet soap is slippery. adjective,* **slip per i er, slip per i est.**

**slump** (slump), **1** drop heavily; fall suddenly: *slump into a chair.* **2** a heavy or sudden fall: *a slump in prices.* 1 *verb,* 2 *noun.*

**sniff** (snif), **1** draw air through the nose in short, quick breaths that can be heard: *The man who had a cold was sniffing.* **2** smell with sniffs: *The dog sniffed at the stranger.* **3** try the smell of: *I sniffed the soup before I tasted it. verb.*

**snout** (snout), **1** the part of an animal's head that extends forward and contains the nose, mouth, and jaws. Pigs, dogs, and crocodiles have snouts. **2** anything like an animal's snout. *noun.*

**soft ball** (sôft′bôl′), **1** kind of baseball game. A larger ball and lighter bats are used in softball than in baseball. **2** ball used in this game. *noun.*

**so lu tion** (sə lü′shən), **1** the solving of a problem: *That problem was hard; its solution required many hours.* **2** explanation: *The police are seeking a solution of the crime. noun.*

**solve** (solv), find the answer to; clear up; explain: *The detective solved the mystery. He has solved all the problems in the lesson. verb.* **solved, solv ing.**

**soothe** (sü͟FH), **1** quiet; calm; comfort: *The father soothed the crying child.* **2** make less painful; ease: *Heat soothes some aches: cold soothes others. verb,* **soothed, sooth ing.**

**sort** (sôrt), **1** kind; class: *What sort of work do you do? I like this sort of candy best.* **2** arrange by kinds or classes; arrange in order: *Sort these cards according to their colors.* **3** separate from others; put: *The farmer sorted out the best apples for eating.* **1** *noun,* **2,3** *verb.*

**sow**[1] (sō), **1** scatter (seed) on the ground; plant (seed); plant seed in: *She sowed grass seed in the yard.* **2** scatter (anything); spread abroad: *The rebels sowed discontent among the people. verb,* **sowed, sown** or **sowed, sow ing.**

**sow**[2] (sou), a fully grown female pig. *noun.*

**squeak** (skwēk), **1** make a short, sharp, shrill sound: *A mouse squeaks.* **2** such a sound: *We heard the squeak of the stairs.* **1** *verb,* **2** *noun.*

**squeak y** (skwē′kē), squeaking: *a squeaky door. adjective,* **squeak i er, squeak i est.**

**squeeze** (skwēz), **1** press hard: *Don't squeeze the kitten, or you will hurt it.* **2** a tight pressure: *She gave her sister's arm a squeeze.* **3** hug: *He squeezed his child.* **4** force by pressing: *I can't squeeze another thing into my trunk.* **5** yield to pressure: *Sponges squeeze easily.* **6** force a way: *He squeezed through the crowd.* **7** crush; crowd: *It's a tight squeeze to get five people in that little car.* **1,3-6** *verb,* **squeezed, squeez ing;** **2,7** *noun.*

**stir rup** (stėr′əp), support for the rider's foot, that hangs from a saddle. See picture. *noun.*

**stoop**[1] (stüp), **1** bend forward: *I stooped to pick up the money.* **2** a forward bend: *She walks with a stoop.* **3** carry head and shoulders bent forward: *The old man stoops.* **1,3** *verb,* **2** *noun.*

**stoop**[2] (stüp), porch or platform at the entrance of a house. *noun.*

**stout** (stout), **1** fat and large: *That boy could run faster if he weren't so stout.* **2** strongly built; firm; strong: *The fort has stout walls.* **3** brave; bold: *Robin Hood was a stout fellow. adjective.*

| | | | | |
|---|---|---|---|---|
| **a** hat | **i** it | **oi** oil | **ch** child | a in about |
| **ā** age | **ī** ice | **ou** out | **ng** long | e in taken |
| **ä** far | **o** hot | **u** cup | **sh** she | i in pencil |
| **e** let | **ō** open | **u̇** put | **th** thin | o in lemon |
| **ē** equal | **ô** order | **ü** rule | **ŦH** then | u in circus |
| **ėr** term | | | **zh** measure | |

ə = { a in about / e in taken / i in pencil / o in lemon / u in circus }

**stroll** (strōl), **1** take a quiet walk for pleasure; walk. **2** a leisurely walk: *We went for a stroll in the park.* **3** go from place to place: *strolling gypsies.* **1,3** *verb,* **2** *noun.*

**sur vive** (sər vīv′), **1** live longer than; remain alive after: *He survived his wife by three years. Only ten of the crew survived the shipwreck.* **2** continue to exist; remain: *These cave paintings have survived for over 15,000 years. verb,* **sur vived, sur viv ing.**

**sus tain** (sə stān′), **1** keep up; keep going: *His cheerfulness sustained us through our troubles. She cannot sustain this pace for long.* **2** hold up; support; bear: *Arches sustain the weight of the roof. verb.*

**swish** (swish), **1** move with a thin, light, hissing or brushing sound: *The whip swished through the air.* **2** make such a sound: *The long gown swished as she danced across the floor.* **3** cause to swish: *The cow swished its tail.* **4** a swishing movement or sound: *the swish of little waves on the shore.* **1-3** *verb,* **4** *noun, plural* **swish es.**

stirrup on a Western saddle

# T t

**thought ful** (thôt′fəl), **1** full of thought; thinking. See picture. **2** careful of others; considerate: *She is always thoughtful of her parents. adjective.*

## thoughtful

**trade** (trād), **1** buying and selling; exchange of goods; commerce: *The United States has much trade with foreign countries.* **2** buy and sell; exchange goods; be in commerce: *Some American companies trade all over the world.* **3** an exchange: *an even trade.* **4** exchange; make an exchange: *He traded a stick of gum for a ride on her bicycle. If you don't like your book, I'll trade with you.* **5** bargain; deal: *I made a good trade.* 1,3,5 *noun,* 2,4 *verb,* **trad ed, trad ing.**

**train** (trān), **1** a connected line of railroad cars moving along together: *A very long freight train of 100 cars rolled by.* **2** bring up; rear; teach: *They trained their child to be thoughtful of others.* **3** make skillful by teaching and practice: *train people as nurses. Saint Bernard dogs were trained to hunt for travelers lost in the snow.* 1 *noun,* 2-3 *verb.*

**truth** (trüth), **1** that which is true: *Tell the truth.* **2** quality or nature of being true, exact, honest, sincere, or loyal. *noun, plural* **truths** (trüŦHZ *or* trüths).

**truth ful** (trüth′fəl), **1** telling the truth: *He is a truthful boy and will tell what really happened.* **2** true; agreeing with the facts: *You can count on her for a truthful report. adjective.*

**tur nip** (tėr′nəp), the large, fleshy, roundish root of a garden plant, eaten as a vegetable. *noun.*

**tusk** (tusk), a very long, pointed tooth that sticks out of the mouth. Elephants, walruses, and wild boars have tusks. *noun.*

# W w

**wedge** (wej), **1** piece of wood or metal thick at one end and tapering to a thin edge at the other. A wedge is driven in between objects to be separated or into anything to be split. See picture. **2** something shaped like a wedge or used like a wedge: *Wild geese fly in a wedge. Their grand party was an entering wedge into society.* **3** split or separate with a wedge. **4** thrust or pack in tightly; squeeze: *She wedged herself through the narrow opening. The hiker's foot was wedged between the rocks.* 1,2 *noun,* 3,4 *verb,* **wedged, wedg ing.**

**wedge** (definition 1)